Living *Life* Awake

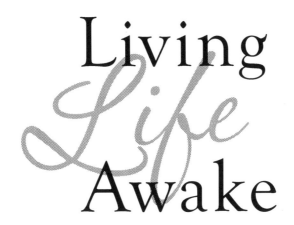

Use Knowledge of the Brain to
Create a Mind Prepared for Your Future

KRISTIN WALKER

ARCHWAY
PUBLISHING

Archway Publishing books may be ordered through booksellers or by contacting:

Archway Publishing
1663 Liberty Drive
Bloomington, IN 47403
www.archwaypublishing.com
844-669-3957

Scripture taken from the King James Version of the Bible.

ISBN: 978-1-6657-0755-8 (sc)
ISBN: 978-1-6657-0756-5 (hc)
ISBN: 978-1-6657-0757-2 (e)

Library of Congress Control Number: 2021910839

Print information available on the last page.

Archway Publishing rev. date: 07/09/2021

Dear reader,

Life, especially as a teenager, has many ups and downs. The good times are awesome, but the bad times and struggles—man, those are the worst! Does your heart ache so badly sometimes that you wonder if you will make it through the day? How can a person hurt so deeply and still exist? Do you wonder why you even exist?

My dear friend, I don't know your particular path, but I can assure you that your path does have purpose and lasting happiness. As you read this book, you will begin to see—to understand—who you are.

For right now, though, I want you to think to yourself, "I am of great worth. I deserve and will feel peace." I know you may not feel this is true, but *it is*. And it is okay if you do not fully believe in yourself right now. That is why I have written this book.

My hope is that after reading this book, you will not be programmed by the world around you. I hope to help you increase in maturity without having to go through the pains typically associated with growing up. I want you to be ready for your own fabulous future. Yes, *your* fabulous future.

Sincerely,
Kristin Walker

To Shae Lynn, Chandler, Brittany, Jesse, Ryan, and Aiden. You have blessed my life; may I always be a blessing in yours.

Welcome to this seventy-five-day journey!

I come to you as

one voice

(a mom's)

sharing

two skills

(how to think with your eyes and feel with your brain),

three questions

(What is my perspective? What is truth? What
actions and thoughts will help me?),

four traits

(humility, reflectiveness, open-mindedness, and dedication),

and

five habits

(thinking, writing, reading, smiling, and overcoming).

The journey of this book began in the late 1990s when I desired to create an immune system for my own soul. I created an article, "Liberty and Happiness for All." I continued to research the brain, and in 2003 I wrote *Think with Your Eyes*. As my understanding of the brain's functions increased and I witnessed the influences in today's cultures, *Living Life Awake* emerged. I felt compelled to share this information in hopes of reaching out to a youth that may be struggling or touching the heart of a youth that doesn't want to wake up one day as a robot. "A robot?" you ask. I'll explain myself in this book. I invite you, now, to take your own journey.

Contents

INTRODUCTION

WHY I HOPE YOU READ THIS BOOK

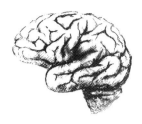

Day 1

Chances are you have a smartphone. You may also have a smart TV or watch. Smart products are everywhere. In this book, I will teach you how to have a smart brain. I'm not trying to insult you. I'm not suggesting you are dumb. The fact is, brains are not designed to be smart. They are designed to help your body survive and exist in a happy state. I'll explain this in more detail later. For now, take the following quiz to see whether you are programming your own smart brain.

Are you programming yourself, or is your life programming you? Take the following quiz to find out.

1. Do you set goals?

    No.—0
    Yes. —1
    Yes, and I write them down. —2

2. If you set goals, do you reflect on them regularly?

    I wish I had the time or could remember! —0
    Yes, I think about them. —1
    Yes, I regularly think about my plans and what I'm doing.—2

3. Do you seek to learn how you can be a better person?

    Sort of. —1
    I actively try to be the best person I can by regularly reading
    or participating in things such as church or extra-curricular
    groups. —2

4. Do you act according to what you *know* is *good*, overcoming
    obstacles?

    No one is perfect, so of course we will all falter at times. On a
    scale of 0 to 2, how easily are you discouraged?

5. Sometimes events and words of others come to us unexpectedly—
    some good, and some not so good. Consider your reactions. Do
    you react to things conscientiously?

    I often regret the things I quickly say and do. —0
    I *try* to control my initial reactions. —1
    I am doing fairly well at slowing down and thinking about what
    is best.—2

The preceding questions are general ones about decisions we make every day. Take, for example, question 4, the question about doing what is good. Each school day morning, how do you wake up? Is it easy for you to get up? Can you get yourself out of bed, or does someone else drag you or nag you out of bed? You know that you must go to school to learn, but how much power do you have to get up? What about your homework? Do you choose to do it without being reminded? You might wish to tell me, "But my homework is hard" or "I don't understand it." Maybe you have a lot of other demanding things to do. Reread question 4 again: "Do you act according to what you know is good, *overcoming obstacles?*" This book isn't a lecture about getting you to do stuff. This book is about helping you achieve what you want to achieve. Among other problems, I'll help you tackle the homework and the "getting up in the morning" issues.

The higher the point value of your answers, the higher your

awareness of your behavior and ability to choose actions you feel are best. As a result, you are programming your life. Save your total score; I will invite you to take this quiz at the end and compare before and after scores. By the end of this seventy-five-day journey, I want you to feel you are in more control of your life and its direction. I want to help you make sure your environment doesn't program your life.

I believe that as tech experts create more humanlike robots and "smart" stuff, our society's culture is creating more robot-like humans. To understand what I mean by this, let's define a robot: a mechanical body that carries out movements according to a program within its frame. Advanced robots can analyze stimuli in the environment to determine which movements or actions it should carry out. Perhaps in the future a robot will be programmed to remember, shed tears, and laugh. What no robot will ever do is decide to perform an action completely different from what it is programmed to do. While humans can be programmed by outside sources, humans *can* change behavior from within.

Before we explore how we can change, let's first consider this question: why would we want to change?

The only real reason to change is to get better results in our lives. Seriously, why change if everything is going well for you? Why change if you know everything you are doing is the best choice for your future?

There is one *really big* problem: we cannot always see the results of our actions until later. This could happen a day or two from now, or a month, year, or several years later. Right now, unless you feel a need to make any changes to your daily life, you assume every action you take is going to get you what you want and need in life. Take a moment right now and write in a notebook what you think you need to change or improve. After all, sometimes we know what we need to do differently. Go ahead. Stop for a moment and think about what you wish to improve.

Now it is time to share one significant fact of life. There is not a single person on the face of this earth that hasn't, after making a decision (even a few days or months later), said, "If I had only known …" or "I wish I had known then what I know now." Have you ever felt that way? Everyone has, and we'll talk about why in this book.

I've told you a problem and a fact. Now I have some questions:

Question 1: What do people wish they had known?

The things people wish they had known in the past varies, of course, but it comes down to this: they thought their actions would yield positive results, and they were wrong. Even if their intentions were good, their knowledge was limited. They didn't have all the information or understanding.

Question 2: Do you think those that made choices that had undesirable consequences felt as if they were making a bad choice at the time the choice was made?

Perhaps sometimes people *do* feel they just don't know what to do and make the best decision they can. Still, whatever the final choices, the person thought those actions were the best. They think, because of what they *do* know, that their decisions were good.

Are you thinking, "But sometimes people know what is best and don't do it?" Bingo. I'm glad you pointed that out. We all do that from time to time. When we choose to do something that we know is not good in the end, we have become trapped by our own bad programming.

Question 3: Are you programming your life, or is life programming you?

How do we change the universal dilemma of poor decision-making and programming? How do we make sure we have all the information and know all the results of choices to prevent poor "programming" and, thus, poor outcomes? How do we change our behaviors for better results?

Take the time to read this book and find out. Learn how to

create a life that you can look back on and live with peace of mind (not a perfect life, though, as no one is going to be perfect). If you really want to have the most rewarding life possible and make those improvements, you are reading the right book.

Don't think I'm picking on you. We are all at great risk of becoming robot-like—yes, *everyone*. Why? because **our society's economy is based on meeting our wants**. In addition, our **brains are set up to**

1. **move us** toward rewards (such as the wants marketed in our society);
2. **protect us from harm**, producing feelings of anger and fear for the fight-or-flight response; and
3. **respond quickly and as easily as possible** using information gathered through life's experiences.

As a result, we are constantly enticed to buy the things we want to have and do things we find pleasurable to do. Unfortunately, what is *immediately desirable* isn't always what will bring the best results in our lives.

Don't be discouraged if you feel you have already made too many mistakes. This book isn't about being perfect; it is about feeling hope and feeling as though life is *worth* living. Let's work on preventing you from spiraling down.

This year, as you read daily from this book, I hope you will

- avoid becoming like a robot,
- develop a smart brain, and
- live life *awake.*

Throughout this book, I will continually encourage you to apply four traits to kindle mature growth. I ask that you

1. be humble by having an attitude of learning from others;
2. reflect upon what you wish to do, how you behave, and the reactions you have;

3. be open-minded by listening; and
4. be committed to what is true and be willing to change what is not, staying true to the real you.

When we adopt the above traits, we start taking control of who we are and who we will become. Whatever your circumstance, this book is a gift to help you in some way. I hope you accept it.

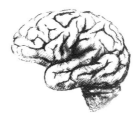

Day 2

What do you want? How are you doing?

Because the purpose of this book is for *your* happiness, the next item of business is vital. Let's talk about *you*. What do you like to do, or what would you like to do in the future? Don't limit yourself to what seems possible or available to you. For example, I wanted to make a quilt several years ago. I had never made a quilt before, so I didn't know whether it would work out. Still, it was something I really wanted to accomplish. What are *you* really interested in?

Below, write what you would like to do now or in the future. Again, do not limit yourself to what is realistic in your eyes.

_____

_____

_____

Write three or more words to describe you.

_____, _____, _____

Write three activities you enjoy in your life.

_____, _____, _____

Write one or more plans or dreams you would like to achieve in the future.

_____, _____, _____

I hope that everything you've written is positive. Do the things you like to do, or would like to do, have positive results in the end? Have you described yourself with positive words?

If for some reason you did not answer the questions above with positive things, we need to have a serious talk. Let me reword that, since a real conversation between us isn't possible. I would like to be of help!

If you don't have a positive view of yourself or your life, this book will help you work through why that is and help you discover how to feel better. If you do have a positive view of yourself and life, this book will help you keep going in a positive direction.

Let's look again at what is in this book.

1. **Discovering What Lies Within:** This pertains to who you are, what you want, and how your brain works. This section will explain the importance of the four traits for kindling change.

2. **Discovering the Lies Within:** This pertains to how the functions of the brain affect us socially and emotionally. It addresses the fact that not every action and emotion coincides with what we truly want to be or achieve. Furthermore, not every thought or belief we have will lead to a positive result. The thoughts and beliefs that allow us—or even force us—to do things that only create problems are "lies." This section contains information about how we become programmed with these lies and explains the four traits necessary for kindling change.

3. **Improving What Lies Within:** This topic will help you "de-robotize" yourself and learn the tools that will allow you to take charge of your own programming. All the thoughts, beliefs, and habits you have developed are programmed in your mind. When we continue to follow what is in our minds and do not change when negative results occur, we have become

like robots. This section will focus on the five everyday habits to improve what lies within.

4. **Stopping the Lies Within from Stopping What Lies Within: The Immune System for the Soul:** Because daily living and de-robotizing yourself can be painful, this information will help you enlist positive feelings to overcome the painful moments. This chapter will focus on the three questions to ask.

Now that you know what lies ahead … ask yourself, "Am I ready to open my mind to new information and my heart to examination? If so, tomorrow we will get started on chapter 1!

1

Discovering What Lies Within

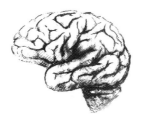

Day 3

Yesterday we talked about you and how you are feeling. In this book I will share with you the difference between you and the real you. The real you is your genuine self—all the traits, skills, and desires that bring you lasting peace of mind and happiness. Genuine desires are important because the real you is still developing and still learning. Remember when I asked you what you want to improve on the first day? This is part of the real you. Your essence is largely based on your biology and environment. Right now, that probably doesn't make sense. In the next few days, we will talk about how we develop as human beings and then examine how this develops your personality and affects the real you. Most importantly, I'll show you how you can program yourself, or take control of your life, to become the real you.

Who Are You?

Some say you are what you eat, and in a way, you are. While there are genetic and biological factors that create you (those that define you as a human, those that you inherit from your ancestors, and those that are unique to you), you have consumed millions of principles, beliefs, experiences, habits, desires, and expectations over the last fifteen years (or however many years you have been alive).[1] Together these factors build your foundation—your programming. Read this paragraph again. Better yet, let me say it again for you.

Some say you are what you eat, and in a way, you are. While there are genetic and biological factors that create you (those that define you as a human, those that you inherit from your ancestors, and those that are unique to you), you have consumed millions of principles, beliefs, experiences, habits, desires, and expectations. Picture a blender. In that blender go ingredients we will call "genes for all humans," and then we will add some "genes from your parents." This is the version of yourself that is born. After you are born, your experiences are added to this mixture each day. Together these factors (this recipe!) build your foundation—your programming.

Do you believe it? To deepen your understanding about your development, this section will explain how your experiences can be compared to eating. Let's look at what you have literally eaten. At first we consume what adults give us. As newborns, we drink milk. As we grow, we have more options and can express preferences. When we are babies, adults respond to our cries; ultimately, the adults make the choices. Gradually, we gain more and more control of what we eat as we grow into adulthood. The same is true about what we consume mentally. We mentally consume by listening, doing, thinking, seeing, reading, and watching. As babies, we have little control over what we hear, see, and experience.

What you have *chosen* to mentally consume has been largely determined by what brings you satisfaction according to what you have already consumed (or "wired") in your life or what has been genetically wired.[2] Later I'll explain what I mean by "wiring."

Let me rewrite that statement for you to read again: What you have *chosen* to mentally consume has been largely determined by what brings you satisfaction according to what you have already consumed (or wired) thus far in your life or what has been genetically wired. There are three reasons why this is true. When you read the next section, keep these three facts in mind:

1. Your brain cannot process information that is not in it.

2. Your brain is biologically wired to seek things that are rewarding and avoid the unpleasant.
3. Your brain sends signals that trigger positive feelings for actions associated with what is already in it.

We all enjoy different activities and have different opinions and viewpoints because we have different experiences in our upbringings and different genetics. If a parent taught me to play basketball and it was an enjoyable experience for me as a child, then I will probably enjoy playing basketball as a youth. It would be a satisfying experience. If in my upbringing I had the opportunity to participate in musical activities and I found doing so was enjoyable, then as a youth or an adult, I will potentially have satisfying experiences associated with music. If my parents, friends, or those around me shared particular political views often while I was a child, those views will influence my views as a youth or an adult. These experiences continue the programming of our brains.

Satisfaction can come in such forms as pleasure, joy, peace of mind, and gratification. In addition to wanting satisfaction regarding nourishment (food), we desire satisfaction regarding physical protection (shelter, for example), emotional needs (feeling loved or cared for), and self-fulfillment (feeling we are doing what we are capable of and what we desire to do).

Consider everything you like to do and can do. Think about your viewpoints. Your life's consumptions, along with your genetic factors, have had an impact on who you are today.

We have consumed (experienced, witnessed, heard, etc.) different beliefs, expectations, habits, traits, values, and hopes throughout our lives. Our brains analyze what we have mentally consumed to determine what will satisfy us. We then behave and think according to the results of the brain's analysis. Let me give you an example. When you get home from school, your mind assesses several options, which may include socializing, chores, homework, or relaxing. You will do what your mind thinks is most rewarding in that moment. If you value getting your work completed, you may do your homework first. If the homework is difficult and stressful, you may choose to first do something relaxing. You may need to talk to a friend about something on your mind. Whatever you choose to do, it is because your mind selected it as the best choice for your happiness in that moment. If your parents taught you to do your homework first and punished you if you didn't, you would be more likely to do your homework first to avoid punishment, even if you didn't really want to do your homework.

Your life experiences have greatly influenced how you think and feel. Your genetics and life experiences have also developed your skills.

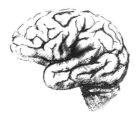

Day 4

Yesterday I told you about how we develop our personalities and skills. Today's section goes into the details of this process—the process of accessing what is in our minds and determining what is most rewarding. You don't have to fully understand this information. This simply explains the science behind your decision-making and your personality. I want you to realize the facts behind the things that can help you improve and control your life.

Biologically, Who Are You? Understanding the Brain

Your brain controls what you think and how you move, speak, and even feel. Logically, then, we can say the workings of your brain are the basis of your personality. The American Psychological Association defines "personality" as the "characteristic patterns of thinking, feeling and behaving." Have you ever thought about the fact that your behaviors, feelings, and thoughts have a pattern? We all have general behaviors, feelings, and thoughts unique to each one of us. Some groups have similar patterns. For example, kindergarteners have similar behaviors that are quite different from those of elderly people. People of the same culture have similar patterns of behavior. These patterns stem from what is in the brain. Yes, for those who believe we have spirits or souls, I believe this too. A supreme being can influence the thoughts in our brains (or our spirits) through the Holy Spirit.

Understanding our brains (minds) is like being health conscious about our hearts and lungs. When we know what helps them function best, we have a greater chance of living a healthy life. Likewise, when we understand our brain's functions, we have a greater chance of living a socially and emotionally healthy life.

Are You Ready to Learn about the Brain? Here We Go

Your brain is a large organ that is part of the body's nervous system. It is nourished with blood and protected by the skull and cerebrospinal fluid. Like all living things, it is made of cells. Brain cells are varied and complex in function; they are the most complicated cells of the body. Luckily, there are just two main kinds of brain cells that you need to know about.

The Parts: The Neurons and the Glia

There are four types of glial cells. These cells guide developing neurons in the early stages of brain growth, protect and nourish neurons, and clean up dying neurons.

Neurons account for only one tenth of the cells in the brain, but they, along with the neurotransmitters (brain chemicals), are responsible for recording how to function (moving, breathing, seeing) and how to act, think, and feel.

But how is it that these materials can translate into a personality and lifestyle?

The Process of Learning

All information enters through the senses: hearing, taste, touch, smell, and sight. (On a spiritual level, a person can receive information from heavenly sources as well. How this exact process works I cannot even pretend to know!) Specific sound waves, light waves, and other signals from the senses activate certain neurons, or nerve cells. Put simply, signals from stimuli in the environment come into cells through their many arms, the dendrites, and out through axons, where cells connect with myriad other dendrites. The signal is passed from cell to cell by chemicals known as neurotransmitters. The signal continues through many other cells. We cannot comprehend the speed at which the electrical signals pass or the number of neurons they pass through.

The more times a particular signal travels through the neuron circuit, the more efficient it becomes in traveling, because glial cells begin to wrap around it, supplying it with a fatty material to insulate it. The resulting covering is known as a myelin sheath. Because of this process, difficult things become easier to do. Also, this process allows one to more easily recall things. Some neurons are so well insulated and efficient that they allow thoughts and information to be quickly recalled, and actions automatically produced. Think about when you first learned to ride a bike; it is difficult at first balancing, pedaling, and steering at the same time. Eventually, with repeated efforts, bike riding becomes easier. This is because your brain is creating efficient neural pathways for this task. The more pathways that your brain develops, especially at a young age, the more effectively it can work and develop new ones.

Signals, of course, come in all the time. Your brain takes in information, and if there is a match for a signal, it travels along its beaten (myelinated) path and eventually manifests itself as a thought, word, or action. Completely new signals must forge a new path. If the signal is not immediately repeated or attended to, the path soon fades away, as if it were never there.

A new piece of recorded information can last for several days, but it takes work to keep it there. Because of this, you can study something and think you know it, and then it is gone (though not before you take the test, I hope!). Additionally, this is why you can change your behavior only to go back to the old ways.

Let me restate the above sentences and add the biological explanation of what happens in your mind. Signals come in all the time. Your brain takes in all this information, and if there is a match for a signal (meaning that the information has already developed an identical or similar pathway), the signal travels along its beaten (insulated with a myelin sheath) path (a neuron circuit) and eventually manifests itself as a thought, word, or action. Completely new signals (such as things you read, see, and hear) must forge a new path (neuron circuit). If the signal (whatever you read, saw, or heard) is not immediately repeated or regularly attended to, the path soon fades (glial cells remove it), and it is as if it were never there. A new piece of recorded information (a stimulus that has created a neuron circuit) can last for several days, but it takes work (attention to the stimulus to keep the neuron connections firing and allowing the myelin sheath to insulate the signal) to keep it there. Because of this, you can study something and think you know it, and then it is gone. In addition, this is why you can change your behavior only to go back to the old ways.

For a piece of information (including actions) to be permanent, it must be repeated a lot. Eventually information and skills are well insulated with a strong synaptic connection; when this happens, we say that such information is a part of our long-term memory. Poorly insulated neurons are subject to decay due to nonuse. Conversely, used neurons become more and more efficient, making thoughts or actions dominating and permanent. In fact, sometimes these dominating thoughts and patterns of behavior make it difficult for new incoming information to receive proper attention.[3] These dominating actions (which include words we say) create the personality we have.

In addition to understanding how our actions, thoughts, and words are produced, understanding this process helps us understand how the environment continues to influence us.

Now do you understand why I keep repeating some of this information? For me to help you learn how to take control of your life, I must influence what is in your brain. How do I do this? By repetition, repetition, and more repetition.

The process of acquiring information, with the interconnectedness of our neurons, can make one thought lead to another. In addition, an action or thought can be triggered by varying stimuli. This happens because the neurons are not isolated cells holding bits of information; they are interconnected, via the dendrites, with countless other neurons. Therefore the smell of something can trigger memories and you can develop "environmentally based" temptations. This is why doing something physical to remember information is effective. In fact, neuron connections that involve the control of movement (learning to ride a bike, for example) are designed for easy and permanent insulation.

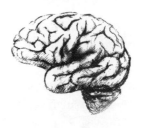

Day 5

Yesterday I described the science behind how we learn and develop habits and skills. Today I will share the brain's process to determine which behaviors and thoughts it will generate. After all, there are so many actions and thoughts you could choose or create. Why do you do and think the things you do and think? Today you will find out! From this information, see if you can figure out why you decide what you do after school each day.

The Process of Behavior and Thought

Incoming stimuli from sensory receptors is changed to an electrical signal and is brought to the thalamus (which is part of the limbic system), where the thalamus begins sending the multiple chains of signals to the other parts of the brain. The signals are then processed in the amygdala (with the aid of the hippocampus and hypothalamus), followed by the prefrontal cortex.

The amygdala gives the brain a chance to detect signals of danger and threats or possibilities of pleasure. If circuits for a significant threat are stimulated, the signal will follow a direct path for action. For example, the adrenal system releases adrenaline and stress hormones. All functions that are not critical are turned off. Blood pressure increases to prepare the brain and muscles for work. The pupils dilate, and the liver breaks down glycogen to prevent an energy crisis. These reactions happen because the body has a response system to protect itself from danger. The body is continually analyzing signals according to the normal standards the brain has established.[4] In addition to monitoring for threats, the mind has been created to ensure reproduction of mankind. Both situations trigger responses that are nearly (if not completely, at times) automatic; a person has little power to overcome intense feelings of fear and physical attraction. These and other strong emotional reactions are wired in the brain stem and limbic system.

The brain stem and limbic system store nondeclarative memory; in other words, the strong neuron connections of these areas cause us to act (and allow organs to work) with little to no thinking on our part. This can be a problem. Thinking is important when it comes to social decision-making. Let's look at the importance of the ability to think, which is the ability to use the prefrontal cortex's working memory. To do so, I want to share with you the story of Phineas Gage. [5]

This is a tragic but true story that took place in 1848. An industrious and well-respected man, Phineas worked as a supervisor for the railroad. Unfortunately, his good work and reputation ended abruptly when a rod struck him in the skull while working. The metal rod went through his brain and removed his left temporal lobe, severing his brain stem from his frontal cortex. Phineas, amazingly enough, regained health; never, however, did he regain the ability to control his emotions or make responsible decisions. Signals came in as they normally do and triggered emotional responses. Because the signals could not reach his prefrontal cortex to retrieve and analyze stored information, and to activate the skills of self-control, social behavior, and delaying needs, Phineas was doomed to act out the behaviors that his brain signaled his body to perform. He was impulsively mad, happy, sad, and fearful. I want to rewrite that sentence for you. Because the signals could not reach his prefrontal cortex, where the signals could be analyzed with stored information and skills in regard to self-control, social behavior, or delaying needs, Phineas was doomed to act out the behaviors that his brain signaled his body to perform.

Understanding the functions of emotions helps us realize the important role they play in our lives. They are not bad influences. Emotions guide our behavior as nerves guide our physical movement. When the brain senses that something is too hot, it will immediately signal the arm or leg to move away. Well, guess what—when the brain senses that something is rewarding or harmful, the brain also signals emotions that help us perform, withdraw from, modify, or maintain a particular action. Pain brings about the desire to fix something. Happiness brings about the desire to keep doing something or to pursue a goal.

We want to create a healthy emotional system that triggers happiness when it is truly a happy option and pain when it is truly a dangerous situation. Right now, you can begin paying attention to how you feel and then think about why you feel that way. What triggered your sad or happy feeling? Why do you feel afraid or mad?

If on day 2 of this journey you wrote or felt negative thoughts about yourself or life, take a moment to think about why. These negative feelings tell you that you want something to change. What do you want to change about yourself or your life? If you have an answer, write it down. We will talk about it later.

One critical but misunderstood response is stress. Stress releases the hormone cortisol. Cortisol aids us in taking action by increasing our heart rates and sugar levels. This is good for circumstances when you need peak performance, such as when giving a presentation, responding in an emergency, or taking a test. Nonetheless, it can be a damaging response. This response, when triggered often, can cause heart problems, back and stomach pain, and weight gain. Just like other neural circuits, the neurons that trigger this response can become well-insulated. That means the slightest stimulus can activate them. For example, if you hate tests, you can have a stress response when a teacher simply says the word "test."

Neuron circuits that accompany emotions are, because of their biological structure, much more effective in producing action than the circuits and systems for producing actions based on the logical decisions of the working memory. As a result, reactions from emotions come faster than reactions from thought. This is because, in times of great danger, your brain does not want you to waste time thinking. Just as in the case of touching a hot stove, it wants you to be ready to act. This is a very useful feature of the brain, but can you see the problem with this setup? We can react before we have a chance to think. This isn't an insult. We are all limited in our perceptions of situations. As a result, sometimes the first reaction isn't the best reaction.

When signals come to the prefrontal area, a more objective analysis of the incoming messages can take place. That simply means you can think more clearly when you do not feel a lot of emotions. This goes for happy emotions as well. Have you ever noticed yourself getting tongue-tied around someone you have a crush on?

The goal of the brain is to respond in a way that will be most rewarding or satisfying. Relevant information is selected to aid in decisions about the best thought or action to employ. Obviously, the information is not literally *selected*. All neuron connections that are related to the issue at hand are activated, and the most rewarding outcome of all the options (of what is stored in the brain) is chosen. Notice that I clarify that the chosen outcome it is not *the* most rewarding outcome; it is the outcome that your brain decides is the most rewarding based on the information available to it. Your brain has access only to information you put in it (or what you receive as inspiration). That is key. Let me rewrite that sentence. Your brain has access only to what comes into it. We will talk about this later, but I want to make certain you understand what determines a reward.

I gave you a ton of information today! As I said earlier, you don't have to understand it completely. I want you to realize that your decisions are based on what is in your brain. And the more you think about or do something, the easier it is to think that thought or carry out that action.

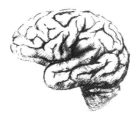

Day 6

In the last few days, we have studied about the brain, our actions, and decision-making. Let me summarize this process today.

Signals come from our five senses. They are quickly analyzed for reward or harm regarding basic human needs and *then* one's unique basic needs—personal and social. If a reward or threat is detected, an emotional response is triggered and we think, say, or do something. If the signals continue, they go through an objective analysis with information in the brain. We think, say, or do what the brain decides is best.

The actual process is very complex and fast because there are multiple signals coming in that activate multiple circuits of varying degrees of insulation. Furthermore, all this is dependent on proper care regarding nutrition, rest, and healthy activity. The brain is an organ; just like the heart and lungs, it has requirements for functioning well.

No matter how complex the process, when all elements of the brain are working properly, the outcome is based upon what is recorded in (or divinely brought into) the brain. When parts of the brain are not working properly, sometimes doctors can prescribe medications to help the brain function correctly.

Two of the most amazing features of the brain are its flexibility and power. These features have been illustrated in numerous recovery stories.[6] Children without the brain matter necessary for sight, learning, and speech have been able to develop these abilities. Just because a skill is not present does not mean it cannot be developed.

It just means it may take more skillful effort and time to develop. Of course, there are limitations to what the brain can do, but most of its limitations are a result of our own limited understanding, time, and resources.

Genetics and human biology provide the framework for our choice of behaviors. Our environments and daily behaviors create circuits that begin to create a "self" (our personality) that those around us come to know. Our genetics and environment do not necessarily help develop the true or *real* you that *we* know or wish to be.

Because this basic understanding is so critical for overcoming the complex problems in our lives, I wish to restate the last two sentences:

1. Our environment and daily behaviors create circuits that begin to create the self (our personality) that those around us come to know.
2. Our genetics and environment do not necessarily help develop the *real* you that *we* know or wish to be.

I love knowing this and find so much pleasure in sharing this truth! Your present or past environment, your past or present circumstances, do not have to define who you are. You can define and be who you are (or want to be) when you choose to take control of your own thoughts and feelings. When you make this choice, you can begin to de-robotize yourself. This does not mean that all your emotions and thoughts right now are bad and that your environment is awful; it means that you will no longer allow yourself to be subjected to crippling negative emotions and poor environmental influences.

We cannot become completely in control in a day. However, I want you to believe that you and I can begin to live our lives fully awake to our circumstances, thoughts, and emotions; and, as a result, we will prevent robotization of poor behaviors and begin the process of de-robotization. I know, I know. I already said that. I want to make sure you heard it.

Let's take a step-by-step look at the difference between living awake and not living awake:

A Robot Person (Not Living Awake)

Biological Processes	Conscious Choices
1. Stimuli come in through all senses. 2. Stimuli are checked for reward or harm. They may immediately trigger an emotion, action, or thought. 3. If an action is not immediately produced, the stimulus is analyzed by information in the brain, via the prefrontal cortex. 4. An action, thought, or emotion is then produced.	A person does whatever he or she feels like doing.

In the above scenario, your action or emotion is determined by whatever your brain thinks is best. Now look at what an awake person does.

An Awake Person

The usual stimuli come in, but notice that the person thinks about his or her behavior. In this way, the person can do better next time.

Biological Processes	Conscious Choices
1. Stimuli come in through all senses. 2. Stimuli are checked for reward or harm. They may immediately trigger an emotion, action, or thought. 3. If an action is not immediately produced, the stimulus is analyzed by information in the brain, via the prefrontal cortex. 4. An action, thought, or emotion is then produced.	The person continually sets goals, reads, talks, and thinks about things that help him or her achieve what he or she wants to achieve or be like. Note: Some people, by virtue of their genetic nature, do this. Others grow up in an environment in which this is taught. 5. The person reflects on the action, thought, or emotion, asking the following questions: Is it truly beneficial? If not, why? How can I change this?

Let me give you a real-life situation. Let's say you come home late from school because of practice. You have homework and chores to do, and you are tired and hungry. What will you do with your time? Your brain will want to relax. When someone reminds you about a chore, this will trigger negative feelings because you are tired and doing chores is not enjoyable. You may feel like yelling "I know!" It is only natural for you to feel negative. Perhaps a friend may text, and you may enjoy talking about what's going on in your lives. If you have electronic games, you may wish to play. You may know in the back of your mind that you have homework, but your brain may think that you still need time to relax. Remember: your brain is constantly thinking of what is most rewarding. Playing a game is more rewarding than homework. Your brain may cause you to decide you can do homework later.

Unfortunately, unless you have someone reminding you of your homework or the chores, your mind may not think about homework for a long time. You'll notice the clock, perhaps, realizing how late it is. What is most rewarding? To just go to bed or do your homework? Unless you feel you *have* to do your homework, you will most likely prefer just going to bed. It may be late into the night that you continue to play the game or talk to your friend before you notice the time. As long as you are enjoying yourself, your brain is happy and will continue to encourage you to play or talk.

But then what happens at school? Will you wish you had taken the time to do your homework?

This is a very generic example. Perhaps you want to do your homework but you don't understand it. In this case, your brain will want to avoid it because it will be painful to do. To succeed, you would have to "teach" your brain that it *is* rewarding to do your homework and that you *can* learn. How do you do that? Keep reading.

The first step is realizing how your brain controls what you do (or don't do!).

If you are the type of person that has no problem doing homework and chores, it is because your brain knows that these activities are good in the long run or sees nothing negative about them.

Here is a pop quiz for you: based on what you've read so far, why is it necessary to live awake, or consciously program your own life? An answer will be examined tomorrow!

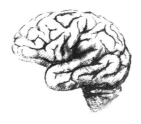

Day 7

Yesterday I asked you, "Why is it necessary to live awake, or consciously program your own life?" Here are some answers:

- The brain isn't very **smart.**
  - The brain can analyze only what is within it.
  - The brain doesn't know all facts or how others feel or what they think.

- The brain isn't very **reliable.**
  - The brain relies heavily on proper care to function well.
  - The brain sometimes remembers inaccurate information, and it doesn't know all things.

When your brain (and mine, and your friends') was developed at birth, it did not have wired in it all the wisdom of the world. In fact, it didn't have the skills to even carry out the basic necessities of life: eating, talking, and walking. It must learn math, reading, and how to drive. We also need to learn effective social skills for interacting and develop the ability to perform the tasks of a job.

Just as the brain and body learn by trial and error in learning to read and do math tasks, they also learn by trial and error for general living. Add to that the fact that the brain is a physical organ with its own limitations in recording and recalling information. And then add to that the limitations the brain has regarding lack of rest or proper nutrition. With these things in mind, it is clear that the brain is *always somewhat unreliable* and sometimes *very* unreliable.

Don't get me wrong. The brain can hold and process information in a way that we cannot fully comprehend. It keeps us breathing without a thought from us. As miraculous as the brain is, it is nonetheless an organ that works in accordance with scientific laws. Fortunately, as has been explained in this book and as you likely know from personal experience, some functions of the brain and body are built to work automatically; others can be made to work automatically, such as language and movement.

Likewise, the same laws apply to the development of habits, beliefs, and expectations. These, too, can become automatic responses. With each reaction and action of the brain, habits are born. From habits are born character and personality—in other words, you. But this you is not entirely the *real* you. That information can be easily overlooked. I'm going to restate this: Some functions of the brain and body are built to work automatically; others can be made to work automatically, such as language and movement. Likewise, the same laws apply to the development of habits, beliefs, and expectations. These, too, can become automatic responses. With each reaction and action of the brain, habits are born. From habits are born character and personality—in other words, you. But this you is not entirely the *real* you.

(If it seemed like I just repeated myself and you have no clue why, it is because your brain started reading words and not paying attention to the message. Seven lines above, I tell you that I'm going to repeat myself. If you caught that, great! If you didn't, this is a great learning opportunity!)

Reflection

1. Think about your abilities, opinions, and preferences.
2. What have you been "given" to read, see, and do (through society, ads and entertainment, school, family, and friends)?

Start paying attention to ads and what the people around you talk about.

3. Think about what you have chosen to read, see, and do. Which books, magazines, and songs do you like?

4. Do you see a connection between your environment and who you are? This is easier to see when you meet others with totally different backgrounds or genetic factors.

Here's another quiz question: why do we think and behave as we do?

I hope your answer was something like this: "Thoughts and behaviors come from the brain's analysis of genetic and environmental information that is physically created in our brains." These thoughts and behaviors become you, which is a mixture of the real you and a socially programmed you.

Now that I have shared the science of how the brain works and how it impacts your development, the rest of this book will be about how we can use this information to our benefit.

Based on what you've learned so far, how do you think this is done? How can we use the workings of the brain to help us?

To improve, we need to change or improve our environment (the things we see, hear, and do). The exact process of how to do this begins in the chapter "Upgrading the Brain's Wiring." For the next few days, before talking about how to make change, I will share with you how the brain can negatively impact your thinking, impacting your ability to change. This will start chapter 2, "Discovering the Lies Within."

2

Discovering the Lies Within

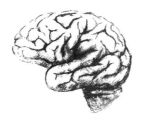

Day 8

In the next few days, I want to explain the three key ideas below:

1. The brain isn't very smart, but the brain doesn't know this.
2. All brains are different.
3. Brains want to be happy *according to what is wired in the brain*.

Today I'll explain the first key idea.

Why Would I Say the Brain Isn't Very Smart? And What Does It Matter if the Brain Knows whether It Is or Isn't?

Synonyms for "smart" include "sensible," "rational," "wise," "logical," and "knowledgeable." For me, when I think of "smart," I think of my friends in school that were always able to get the right answers. They just seemed to have the ability to quickly learn the right way to work out math or chemistry problems.

All brains work with varying abilities, but even the brains of the smartest of people do not have access to all information. I'm referring to more than social studies, math, and science facts here. I'm referring to

- knowledge of what is in the minds of all persons,
- the ultimate outcomes of all actions or thoughts, and
- the inherent ability to perform all success-promoting tasks and habits.

In other words, in a given moment, a person may be limited by experience or knowledge in making a decision or reacting to what has happened. We are not limited in all things, of course. We gain knowledge and understanding as we grow up, even throughout adulthood. Still, there never comes a time when we are omniscient and completely capable of all things we wish to do.

Understanding this fact is critical. If a person thinks he knows everything, or if a person simply does not realize that he needs to evaluate his own thoughts and behaviors, that person will always do what he believes to be the best decision and will do what feels right or easy.

Let me repeat that statement and break it apart for easier evaluation.

If a person
thinks he knows everything
    or does not realize that he needs to evaluate his own thoughts
    and behaviors,
then that person will always
do what he believes to be the right decision
and will be at risk of
doing only what feels easy to him.

Certainly, our goal is to make all the tasks that are best feel right and easy to do. In the meantime, "feels right" and "easy" are sometimes also "Brings satisfaction now" and "takes the least amount of work." This concept is apparent in very young children who are still learning the benefits of work and delayed gratification. For example, cutting, drawing, and cleaning are continual struggles for four-year-olds that I work with. These tasks are necessary but are not easy to develop. Giving up, however, isn't the best decision. You may struggle as you learn new things too. Sometimes you may feel like giving up. Would we learn anything new or get better at our hobbies if we gave up all the time? What if you gave up the first time you messed up in a video game? You would never win any game if you quit each time you made a mistake!

Learning how to react when something is disappointing is another major struggle for young children; the immediate reaction is anger or sadness. They must learn to focus on solving the problem rather than wasting time reacting negatively to it. Learning to problem solve or move on when you are feeling a negative emotion is *not* easy.

Even among adults, no one is perfectly capable or knowledgeable in all things. If a person does not reflect upon his own thinking and behaviors and habits but chooses instead to continue through life doing as he feels is best in any given moment, his success is subject to environment and genetics. The person has no real control. The only changing factor would be the environment. Sometimes a person's environment and genetics are favorable. Because of this, positive outcomes can be naturally achieved for certain periods of time in a person's life.

But no one's life easily provides all the necessary opportunities toward goodness and ultimate reward. We are all limited, to some degree. No one's environment or genetics provides an easy course to never-ending happiness. There are many examples of this; I will share just a couple. Albert Einstein, as an example, was born with great cognitive abilities. Considered the most influential physicist of the twentieth century, he is famous for the equation E=mc2. He, however, had family and financial problems.

Famous singers that become drug addicts provide another example. They have a natural ability to perform and an environment favorable enough to bring fame. Why would people that achieve a lifetime dream and have a life of luxury need to take drugs? Perhaps it is not a need but a want. They can afford the drugs. If this is the case, why would they want to go to rehabilitation centers to stop? We can safely assume in such cases that these famous artists later learned it was not a good decision to start taking drugs in the first place. Whether they started for simple pleasure or to escape problems, it was still a poor decision that was not easy to overcome. They did not have the foresight to know *not* to start.

In the first example, we see that cognitive intelligence alone does not ensure happiness and success in all things. In the second, we see that achieving a dream and having money does not ensure happiness and wisdom.

Sometimes limited thinking effects decisions made as a group, such as with the making of the famous "lemon sucker" car, the Edsel.[7] Years ago, Ford spent numerous hours and dollars on the preparation and marketing of a car. It failed miserably. The company—or at least a portion of upper management—was confident of its success. They were wrong. Had they known the outcome, they would have made different choices. Their brains were limited in knowledge and perspective.

Our perspectives will always be limited. We will always make mistakes.

What is the answer to this dilemma? There are four of them, actually:

1. Have an attitude of learning.
2. Be reflective.
3. Be open.
4. Be committed—willing to change while staying true to the real you.

Read the above items again. What do you notice about them? These are not specific truths about how to be happy. These are ways of learning the truths of happiness.

I will bring these points up again and again. For now, I hope you are convinced that you do not know all things that are for your good, for your happiness and success.

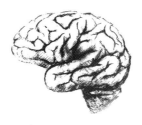

Day 9

We are on topic 2 of the three key ideas I want to share:

1. The brain isn't very smart, but the brain doesn't know this.
2. All brains are different.
3. Brains want to be happy according to *what is wired in the brain*.

All Brains Are Different

"All brains are different" probably seems like a stupid statement to make. Of course brains are different! However, our knowing this as a fact and our relating it to our interactions in life are on two different brain circuits.

There is one common characteristic of all brains: imperfection! Brains are imperfect in different ways. This is why it is important not to compare them. Everyone has strengths and weaknesses. Some brains are cognitively skilled. Others are emotionally and socially skilled.

It is not necessarily a fact that every person you will encounter will have a strength you do not have. The fact is, it is important to understand that others have knowledge, perspectives, and skills that you do not. The most important thing to realize is that there is not a single human brain with the capacity to understand the perspectives and background experiences of all other people.

Remember, too, that you have strengths that others might not see. You may be tempted to see others' strengths and not value your own. Why is this important to realize? Remember: our thinking influences the way we behave and interact.

When children develop theory of mind, their behavior changes. They start to recognize opinion and perspective. They talk to others about conflicts, share feelings, and accept the opinions of others more easily.

As adults, we know that people are different, but sometimes we don't fully realize the extent of our differences. In addition, we can have the wrong understanding of *how* brains are different. As a result, we can develop negative viewpoints.

To aid you in understanding others, I have listed various personality types social experts have identified. These descriptions only scratch the surface, of course. You can learn more from other books, but the main idea is to realize that people truly have different perspectives, backgrounds, skills, and patterns of behaviors.

Some social experts describe four basic types of personalities: sanguine, choleric, melancholic, and phlegmatic. We have personalities with combinations of these types, and every personality type has its strengths and weaknesses. Below I describe these types neurologically, according to my perspective and research.

Phlegmatics are people whose brains have a need for social connections and have strong neurological pathways and chemicals that produce optimistic feelings.

Choleric personalities belong to people whose brains have a strong need for making sure things happen. Thus, they tend to lead and want to be in control. They have a strong sense of self and their plans. Because of this, they tend to have strong neurological pathways that produce feelings of anger when plans do not go as they intend.

Melancholic people have brains that have a strong need for order, purpose, meaning, and understanding. They are more likely to be analytical. They have relatively strong connections regarding emotions that produce sad feelings.

Sanguine people's brains have a need for freedom, pleasure, and adventure. They have strong neurological connections for emotions that produce feelings of happiness.

Another way social scientists depict personality is by analyzing the following elements:

- energy level
- rhythmicity
- approach or withdrawal to new experiences
- adaptability to changes
- sensitivity to sounds, smells, and lights
- intensity of emotional reactions
- quality of mood: typically optimistic or pessimistic
- potential for distraction
- attention span and persistence

Personality can also be defined by looking at the elements of the Myers-Briggs test listed below. You can research these varying types of personalities.

Myers-Briggs

Extroversion vs. Introversion: This trait describes how a person gets his or her energy. Do you know friends that love being with other people? Do you know people that prefer to be by themselves?

Sensing and Intuition: This trait explains how you and your friends gather information. Do you or others you know rely only on facts and what can be physically examined? Do you know anyone that relies on spiritual insights?

Thinking and Feeling: This facet of personality explains how we process information. Do you use logic to make decisions, or do you make decisions based on feelings?

Judging and Perceiving: This part of the personality describes how you and your friends implement your decisions. Do you plan things out, or do you improvise?

Three other unique aspects of each person are the following:

- knowledge/skills—natural abilities and those gained by formal training
- interests—as a result of either natural abilities or desires to develop abilities
- perspective—beliefs about life and circumstances based on one's own experiences

The reason I am talking to you about differences among brains is to help yours! Your brain thinks its own way of working is right. Even if you think you are stupid, your brain thinks that it is right in thinking that you are stupid. Let's say someone else encourages you to try something that is difficult. What do you say? "No, I can't do that." Maybe you don't say that. I don't know. Maybe you always have a good attitude and think, "Yeah, maybe I can do that" every time you fail. If you can do that, that is incredible. So many books have been written to help people not get discouraged. Why is it so hard not to be discouraged? Not being discouraged goes against what your brain has said is true. Your brain sees you fail and says, "That's it. You're done. You can't do this."

Your brain also makes decisions about others. I hope this section has helped you see that people can have different viewpoints, skills, experiences or memories, and interests. Your brain needs to learn this truth. Otherwise, your brain (mind) will perceive events and the behaviors of others incorrectly.

Remember the 4 Traits?

Trait 3 is "be open-minded." This does not mean you accept what everyone says and does. This means you can be cautious about accepting your own immediate perceptions. This means you can seek to learn from others.

This also means that your own perspective and skills are essential for group progress. Because everyone has a different perspective of things, your friends may not see or understand what you do. Your perspective may provide important insight, or it may not. The fact is, you cannot assume it doesn't matter. Likewise, no one can always assume his or her own viewpoint is accurate.

You can use this information to help you in so many situations, including school, work, and home life. Several leaders teach that you can get rid of stress or stop yourself from reacting poorly if you reframe the situation you are in. For example, Steven R. Covey tells a classic story about an unruly child that disturbs travelers on a train while the father ignores the child. Irritated, a passenger complains to the father. Irritation immediately melts to sympathy when the passengers learn about the family's sad story: the children just lost their mother. The child's behavior did not change; the perspective of the situation changed.

I'm letting you know that the mind does not always have an accurate idea of the situation and we can decide to seek out more information before we react.

Changing our perspectives helps us to feel better. However, sometimes a situation is truly challenging. If you feel bad about something, you have the right to feel as you feel. You can respectfully share how you feel. Also, if someone around you is not happy, there is a reason for that. The problem may simply stem from an inaccurate perspective. You may want to find out the facts before making assumptions. Feel comfortable in sharing your feelings, and be open to listening to others' feelings.

> When we fully understand that all brains
> are different, the following happens:
>
> 1.   Leaders seek, as much as is possible, to understand the perspective of everyone involved.
> 2.   Coworkers and family members are mindful of one another's feelings and opinions. Coworkers and family members feel safe to express feelings.
> 3.   The skills and knowledge of each person are respected in group environments.

Today's message is about how we are all different. This makes life difficult at times, but the differences we have are necessary. We need one another's' skills and knowledge.

Before I end the message for today, it is important to address the fact that sometimes people's brains can have imperfections in how they function. This means that emotions can be triggered even without connected stimuli in the environment or perhaps that some people's emotions can be stronger or weaker than those produced by the typical brain. For these situations, medicines help the brain function normally. Nevertheless, these brains still go through the same processes, and persons with the imperfections in the functions of the brain—even with the medicines—are still subject to the imperfections caused by lack of development of the brain that everyone experiences. Remember the story I shared about Phineas Gage? His brain was physically damaged, and its ability to function well was permanently altered. All of us have the same problem as he did, to some degree, but what was physical damage to neuron connections for him is only underdevelopment of neuron connections of correct truths and behaviors for us.

Additionally, differences in firing (the passing of signals from one neuron to another), the brain's ability to form myelin sheathing to insulate neurons, and the amounts of neurotransmitters released and taken back up after a firing (among other varying factors) affect emotions and learning capabilities.

I hope reading this message has helped you appreciate yourself and others around you. You are important, and it is okay that you are not perfect.

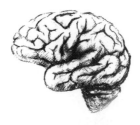

Day 10

We are on topic 3 of the three key ideas I wanted to share. Do you remember what they are?

1. The brain isn't very smart, but the brain doesn't know this.
2. All brains are different.
3. Brains want to be happy *according to what is wired in the brain.*

Let's begin our exploration of this idea.

Brains Want to be Happy According to What is Wired in the Brain

Studies have shown—and life itself is evidence of the fact—that all behavior is a result of the brain's desire to make the owner happy in a given moment. As a result, rewards have become popular in school. Initially, in the history of formal schooling, punishment (such as the dunce hat) was used to scare children into good behavior. When psychologists learned about the real impact of "reward," schools gave out all kinds of tangible rewards to lead children into good behavior. And then came the realization that children need to behave well according to internal rewards and not external, tangible rewards. Figuring out how to help a child internally appreciate doing something hard *now* for rewards that are far in the future is very difficult. Even as adults, it can be difficult! Have you ever tried to improve your health, save money, or quit a bad habit?

We need to consider two aspects of statement 3:

1. The <u>goal</u> of the brain is happiness.
2. <u>What is wired in the brain</u> determines how happiness is achieved.

The Goal of Happiness

Take a moment and think about happiness. When have you been happy? Why? As you think about happy moments, you will probably realize there are many kinds of positivity: peace of mind, relief, joy, excitement, laughter, etc. Some moments of positivity are short, and some last a long time. This may seem like a useless observation, but it is important to point out. The brain is limited to what is wired in it, and it (the brain) wishes to have positivity all the time. The brain is designed that way.

Therefore, in a given moment, a person may make a choice based upon what will bring positivity for a short period of time but bring misery afterward. Maybe this has happened to you or someone you know. For example, it is easy to relax and chat with friends instead of preparing for a test. However, when you take the test, you may wish you had studied. I recall, as a Spanish teacher, hearing one of my students mumble, "Man, I've got to learn to study for these tests." And that was prior to his last test of the year! Of course, not all short moments of positivity are bad; the enjoyment of a movie, an activity with a friend, and the reading of a book are all good experiences. I want you to understand that some moments of positivity may bring problems in the long run. Because of this, we must consciously desire to want long-term positivity. We want to make decisions that will bring about good feelings that will last.

Sometimes you may need to make a decision that has short-term negativity, such as resisting the temptation to eat a candy bar or pushing yourself to go to the gym. It isn't much fun resisting the urge to eat tempting foods or exerting energy to exercise. We do these things only because they are "good for us."

The important point to understand today is that there are different time frames for achieving happiness. The most ideal positivity to want is a lasting one, and sometimes we must be willing to accept and endure some degree of negative feelings in order to obtain a higher level of positivity.

For example, saving money for something special takes some patience and requires moments of denying oneself an immediate reward. You must deal with feelings of disappointment when you cannot have something you want right now, knowing you will later be excited to purchase it. If you spend money on little things that you are momentarily interested in, you will not have the money later. The same idea goes for dieting, exercise, and controlling emotions, and the list goes on.

Whatever your goals, your mind wants to be happy.

Now let's move on to part 2 of today's topic—how your brain achieves the goal of happiness.

According to What Is Wired in the Brain

Your brain is an organ. *Your* organ. Just as your muscles can do only what your muscles are capable of and your heart can function only according to the physiology of your circulatory system, so too does your brain function according to its physical structure.

This may seem like another absurd statement to make. *Of course* you make decisions according to what is in your brain! A better way to look at it is this: We can access only what is in our own brains (or what is brought via inspiration into our minds). Our brains do not have access to all knowledge and skills in the world. Changing behavior requires changing the mind. Remember: your brain can produce the best of behaviors only if the information and behaviors are recorded on well-insulated circuits. Review the section about the brain, if necessary, to remember this process.

We do things that are the most rewarding of all the options *in a given moment and according to the brain.*

And just *how* does the brain determine which things are the most rewarding? The most rewarding option in each situation is the most well-insulated neuron circuit that has produced positive feelings closely connected with the stimulus of the given circumstance. Whoa. That is a mouthful! In a moment of making a choice, your brain fires up circuits related to your experience. You notice this by way of your thoughts. Your mind will think most easily about the options that you usually use. Your mind will not be able to even consider all the options; it can consider only those that it knows about.

Let me give you an example. Let's say it is the beginning of the year and you decide you want to lose ten pounds. You go out to a movie with a friend. As you pass the ticket stand and head for the theater, you pass the concessions. Eating popcorn will not help you with your goal. What do you choose to do? If you never buy popcorn and soda, there will not be a neurological pathway for this behavior, and passing it up will be easy. If you typically purchase popcorn, you will be tempted. In other words, previous experiences will be activated, and you will remember the reward of eating popcorn.

Will you get popcorn or not? The overall outcome will be dependent on several factors:

- What is most important to your brain in that moment?
- Are you hungry?
- How important is your goal?
- How strong is your memory of the enjoyment of eating popcorn?
- Do you have the necessary money?

All of this is analyzed by the brain as it searches for the best option. The hungrier you are, the less energy you will have to resist a temptation. *The brain will fight for your "survival."* The less resolved you are in your goal (in other words, the less insulated the neuron circuit for your goal is), the more pull your desire for eating popcorn will have (in other words, your brain will know that positive feelings will be produced by eating the popcorn, and it will provide the motivation to do that). After all, in that quick walk past the concessions, the greatest reward the brain really knows about is eating popcorn. It has not seen a reward (weight loss) from *not* eating popcorn.

On the other hand, let's imagine it is the beginning of the year and you have decided you are going to lose ten pounds. You wrote down the goal and decided which eating behaviors you would have to change. You have thought about how wonderful it will be when you can once again fit in your favorite pair of Jeans or feel healthier again. You went to the store and purchased healthy snack items to have on hand. With all these actions and thoughts, you have created a neuron circuit with "losing weight" as the reward in mind.

When you go to the movie and pass by the concessions, you may be tempted. However, because you have a strong sense of reward for losing weight, the reward you have for eating popcorn pales somewhat in comparison. You keep thinking about your goal as you walk past the popcorn stand. You come out victorious! The next time you are in such a situation, your brain will have a moment of victory in its storage, which will help you decide what is best. Thus, your experience has created the potential for it to be a little easier to choose what you ultimately wish to do the next time around.

Eating buttery popcorn is not bad. It doesn't harm anyone else or the environment. In fact, it tastes absolutely delicious! If you want to lose weight and be healthy, eating popcorn just doesn't help you achieve your goal.

Start paying attention to the decisions you make. Do you do what you really want to do, or are you controlled by habits? Habits are well-insulated circuits that produce an immediate positive feeling.

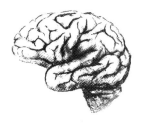

Day 11

In chapter 1 (the first week), I shared the very biological processes of the brain; then, in chapter 2, I began sharing how the processes of the brain impact our lives. Our genetics, backgrounds, and cultural experiences have created neurological circuits of lies regarding what will bring you the greatest happiness. Not everything in your mind is accurate about what will bring you the best reward. Not everything your brain perceives, or thinks is correct. Because of this, I hope you seek to live life more consciously. Remember:

- *The brain isn't very smart.* It can analyze only what is within it. It doesn't know all facts or how others feel or what they think.
- *The brain isn't very reliable.* It relies heavily on proper care to function well. It sometimes remembers inaccurate information and doesn't know all things.

In the coming days, I will share statements that provide further understanding of the "lies" in your mind and the steps of living life awake. *The first two truths* are widely accepted among psychologists, statements 3, 4, and 7 are deduced from science research, and statements 5 and 6 are scientific facts about the brain.

1. We have many social habits recorded.

2. We have expectations and habits and personality traits recorded.
3. Everything recorded in your brain is established as normal or as truth until opposing stimuli are recorded and accepted.
4. Emotions are a result of the brain's analysis of new stimulus; they motivate or stop us.
5. Everything is relative.
6. Emotional responses fade.
7. The brain is built for efficiency. A blunt way of saying this is "The brain is lazy."

Take a moment today to write down any discouraging thoughts you have had recently. We will look at why we have negative thoughts in the coming days as we examine the seven statements above.

Keep paying attention to the decisions you make and the thoughts you have.

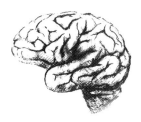

Day 12

Have you paid attention to your thoughts, feelings, and decisions? Have you wanted to do something but then were afraid to do it? Did you feel you couldn't do it?

Today we will look at the first two truths about the brain that expose the lies it can create! Your brain doesn't purposely lie to you. Your brain simply doesn't know everything, but it doesn't know that it doesn't know everything! So your brain makes decisions using the limited knowledge stored in it. As a result, you may think you can't or shouldn't do something. Sometimes you think you aren't good enough to do things. Sometimes you think something is bad when an experience or opportunity is, in reality, good for you, or the other way around. Let's jump in and start talking about how this happens.

We Have Many Social Scripts or Habits Recorded or "Consumed"[8]

(See "Who Are You?" from day 3 to refresh your memory about how experiences are recorded in our brains.) Some habits are unique to us. Some scripts are unique to gender, age, or socioeconomic background. Others are common among certain cultures or religious upbringings. These scripts were gradually recorded in the brain as we grew up.

I see what my guardian, family, and friends do. The things the people in my life do often becomes recorded. This becomes a part of me but may or may not necessarily correlate with the real me. I see others around me. I hear them. I learn from them. I go to school and learn from my peers as well. I observe things around me: advertisements, music, news, and entertainment. I see how others are dressed and what others want. I hear their language. I make connections as the signals pass from neuron to neuron. I begin learning what I can expect from life and others, and what others expect of me, and I experiment with getting or doing what I want. I begin to establish "me," but (again) not necessarily the real me. I experience life, and my brain responds according to (1) what has been in it from birth, (2) what I put in my brain by way of my choices, and (3) what my environment puts in my brain because of repeated exposure.

Here are some examples: I know what acceptable behavior is in school. (I may or may not choose to behave acceptably, but I know what is expected!) I know what all the traffic signals mean. I know how to say "Hello, how are you today?" when I see someone. In a job interview, I know it is good to give a good, firm handshake. I know to say "Excuse me" when I sneeze. These examples may seem like simple things, but you must remember that cultures are different. Shaking hands is appropriate because it has been established in our culture as good, not because the shaking of hands itself is such an honorable gesture. In fact, in the year 2020, with the invasion of the novel coronavirus, shaking hands became an undesirable custom.

Throughout the centuries of humankind's existence, social dialogues and norms have been challenged and often changed, though not easily. Slavery was acceptable, children were told to be seen and not heard, and women were not allowed to go to school or permitted to vote.

We have individual scripts too. Just like social ones, they can change as we experience and learn throughout life.

The great tragedy is that our true selves can get lost, buried, or forgotten because of this self that has been socially developed over the years by culture, media, and marketing.

We Have Expectations, Habits, and Personality Traits Recorded[9]

Some of the recordings, or scripts, that we follow are not true-self expectations, because they initiate actions that are unsatisfactory in the long run.[10] Others are neither good nor bad; they are simply different from those of others around us.

This truth was introduced and explained earlier. (See "Our Brains are Different" from day 9.) When our recordings (expectations and traits) are different from those of others in our social and work environments, problems *can possibly* develop; the next truth explains why problems can arise in such situations.

Before moving on, however, let me make a list of what is physically stored in your brain, in a complex system:

- expectations of what you value, believe, and want (in the form of values, beliefs, principles, and goals)
- habits
- personality traits

As you paid attention to your thoughts and choices, did you notice any patterns? Do any thoughts keep coming into your mind? Are there any actions that wish you could stop doing? Do you see why you have repeating thoughts and why it is hard to quit habits? Your brain is constantly firing along neural circuits in your mind.

Day 13

Yesterday I mentioned that having different expectations or personalities could cause problems. This next truth explains why this happens.

Everything Recorded in Your Brain Is Established as Normal or as Truth until Opposing Stimuli are Recorded and Accepted

In other words, you will always feel you are right about everything you think. This is one of the most important truths to know, understand, and remember! Every person in this world has ideas he or she thinks is right. What happens when people with two opposing ideas work together? A major conflict! Their abilities to handle opposing ideas will affect how they react and resolve the issue. Young children have a very difficult time with conflict because they don't understand this truth.

Earlier I explained the fact that our brains are different. Theory of the mind—the ability to understand that each person has his or her own mind—is developed as we grow. In other words, it is a developed skill of the brain to recognize that others have a brain that is different from our own. Infants don't even realize that they are entities that are separate from the rest of the world. While we are all connected socially and can have impacts on our environment and vice versa, we are not so connected that we have total control of or insight into everything. As we grow, we learn we are separate and unique.

However, your brain considers all the unique beliefs and personality traits and habits that you have recorded as correct, good, and moral—in other words, *right*. This is not a bad design of the brain. In fact, your immune system does the same thing. Your body learns what your personal cells are like and attacks anything different. The only healthy way (and practical, for that matter) for your body and mind to function is with the assumption that "self" is good. Furthermore, because our true identities coincide with truth, goodness, and happiness, we *want* our true selves to be normal. We want it to be easy to do what will be best in the long run.

Unfortunately, we are not born with the abilities and knowledge of everything good; and then, on top of that, we learn false ideas through our upbringing and develop traits that are not always associated with truth, goodness, and happiness. As a result, it is sometimes hard to know what is honestly good in the long run and what is not.

Among the many things the brain establishes as normal are the way you live, the things you eat, the beliefs you have, the expectations you desire, and the habits and personality you've developed. Anything different, unless you learn (neurologically record by experience) otherwise, seems wrong, strange, or impossible (or produces some other negative feeling). Even if we have an attitude of humility, we still have a brain that is egocentric. It thinks it is right. It knows no different unless we tell it so. To "tell" it is to have an experience or learn something that opens our minds. (You will learn later how to teach your brain what is right). In summary, not only do we each have a basic script that we live by, but we also perceive the script to be correct.

Consider the hardship of addictions, in which the brain has learned to survive and adjust its makeup according to the drug a person has consumed. When the person tries to quit, the brain reacts very negatively during the withdrawal stage; it does not believe the body can survive without the substance. The person then feels unable to survive without the very item that is threatening his or her life.

This aspect of the brain affects us all, not just those trying to break from addictions. The brain can cause people to be wrongfully confident or pessimistic. For example, perhaps I am genuinely not capable of carrying out a task, but my brain thinks I can. (This is not to say that I cannot learn to do it; I just can't do it now.) If I think I can and fail in my attempt, I risk becoming depressed and thinking that I'm a failure. Worse yet, if I'm overly confident, I may cause risk for myself or others. Teenagers, for example, can engage in risky behaviors because their brains have not fully developed the ability to process necessary information. Have you heard stories about classmates doing things that have been harmful? On the other hand, if I devalue my skills or capabilities, I may avoid opportunities that can be fulfilling for me or helpful to others. I may perform in a way that communicates poor ability and reinforces how I perceive myself.

This is one reason why I wanted to write this book. All of us are still growing and learning, but while you are a teenager or young adult, your brain is still developing biologically. Your mind doesn't know this. Even as you read this, you may be thinking, "What is she talking about? Does she think I'm an idiot?" No, teenagers are not idiots. Teenagers simply don't have complete access to their prefrontal cortex. It isn't that teenagers can't make responsible choices. It is that they are less inclined to notice or think through all the facts of a situation. Teenagers are also more likely than others to react emotionally.

A tragic example of the brain's design to accept what is in it as reality can be seen in the case of trauma victims. When the brain picks up signals that are similar or identical to the signals that preceded or coincided with a bad event (such as a car wreck), the brain triggers the body to act as if it will happen again. Even if the situation is perfectly safe, the brain believes it is in either emotional or physical danger.

The brain will behave in the same manner on less weighty matters. Cultures, for example, have established what is normal for public behavior, youth and adult behavior, apparel, punishments for crime, family traditions, and social customs. Some of these norms bring about positive results; others may not.

The damage caused by differing perceptions is most apparent in marriages, where differences of norms may clash. Unless a couple takes the time to discuss their perspectives, the differences can become conflicts. Each person may not understand that the other truly views the situation differently. According to their background, they may be doing what is correct or acceptable. (Though there are times when a spouse may do something contrary to what is right, even by his or her own viewpoint.)

Established norms in our own brains are often correct (meaning they will produce positive or neutral results). As we grow up, we gain further insights. Not all the norms (expectations, goals, habits) of our lives and our society need to be changed. The point is that some do.

With so many social platforms and ways to connect, the social world can be excruciating! What if someone doesn't reply right away? Is he or she mad at you? Is he or she rude? Is something wrong? Is the person okay?

Your brain is also influenced by the onslaught of pressure to make trendy purchases. Your mind begins to believe you must have the latest things to be accepted or to socially excel. How do you feel when you don't have what others have?

I invited you to start paying attention to your thoughts, decisions, and behaviors. Do you react negatively or quickly sometimes? Do you feel sad easily? Being a teenager is tough! I still have my journals from when I was a teenager. I got mad about some terribly silly things in those days. At the time, I didn't think they were silly.

Don't get discouraged. Every adult was a teenager once, and every adult is still growing. Keep reading and I'll help you start controlling your brain and life instead of your brain controlling you.

Knowing what I just taught you will help a lot. Take a deep breath when someone says something different from what you believe and start talking through conflicts.

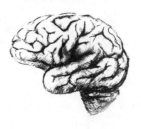

Day 14

So far, I've explained the following ideas:

1. We live by scripts.
2. These scripts include expectations, habits, and personality traits.
3. These scripts are established as normal and correct by our brain's functioning.

What happens at a neurological level when the brain encounters something contrary to one of our recorded scripts? That was a technical way of saying, "What happens in our brains when we don't get what we expected?" (Perhaps we don't do well on a test, someone says something negative to us, or we step in a mud puddle.)

Truth 4 provides the answer: *emotions are a result of the brain's analysis of a stimulus and act as a motivator for action.* The brain uses existing circuits for this analysis. Some existing circuits are those wired from birth, such as those that analyze physical threats and those responsible for reproduction. Today I will tell you about truth 4 in two parts: the negative responses and the positive responses.

There Is a Negative Response when a Stimulus Conflicts with another Existing Circuit

A study by Schultz et al. (1997) shows a decrease in the release of dopamine when an expected reward is denied. Dopamine is one of the neurotransmitters of the brain that serves a function as it passes the signal from one neuron to another. Dopamine's role is motivation and sensing reward. At the time of denial of an expectation, this neurotransmitter decreases its normal firing rate.

As a result of the brain's system, a person whose brain decreases the firing rate of dopamine ends up feeling an emotion we typically interpret as negative. Emotions come in varying degrees, depending on how contrary the stimulus is. This may include feelings of anger, frustration, hopelessness, depression, or sadness. For example, if I have certain expectations in a relationship and something happens that is contrary to these expectations, I may feel angry. Or, if I believe in something (political or moral) and I hear or experience something that conflicts with that belief, I may feel sad or scared. If I even *wish* to do something contrary to any circuit in my brain—even if I know that circuit relates to a habit I want to eliminate—I will have negative emotions. This is because the actions I wish to take are contrary to existing circuits. Yes, even if I have a recorded expectation or a goal that will produce negative results, thinking or acting contrary to what is in the brain in hopes of getting positive results will produce negative emotions. (Remember the example of addictions.)

Let me write that message again: *everything* that conflicts to the *slightest* degree with what the brain has recorded creates a negative reaction of some degree. This is the second-most-critical fact to understand for human improvement. The natural degree of negativity varies among people as well. In other words, some people naturally feel worse than others when the same negative event occurs.

People can learn to control negative feelings. We call this "self-regulation" in early childhood education. Generally, it is called "maturity." A mature child (or adult) responds appropriately to conflicting stimuli.

Let me take that last statement apart:

- *mature*—displaying outstanding behavior based on cultural expectations
- *responds appropriately*—reacts, behaves
- *to conflicting*—anything different from his or her own point of view or expectations
- *stimuli*—things seen, heard, or experienced

Let's say a child falls and hurts his or her knee. It is acceptable for a child to cry in our culture; the knee causes pain as the result of a natural process of the body. We would say the young child is mature if he or she were to get up and say, "I'll be okay, Mommy. Can we go clean it and get a Band-Aid to stop the bleeding?" If, however, a school administrator fell and hurt his or her knee to the same degree, we would be surprised if the adult sat down and cried. Wouldn't you think your school administrator was pretty immature? We all would expect that an adult would understand that wounds hurt, tolerate the pain, and take care of it.

Negative reactions can be healthy though. If we never experienced fear or anger, we would never protect ourselves or others from danger or problems. Your body pulls away from heat because the brain has established a norm for the degree of heat it will allow itself to encounter. In much the same way, our brains compare outside information with what they know (have recorded via neuron circuits) and react negatively when stimuli (things we experience and see) are different from what is recorded in them. Negative reactions give us the motivation to change ourselves or things in our environment.

A stimulus can be considered good and bad (from the brain's perspective) when there are neuron connections that support differing results. For example, a new exercise habit can be analyzed as good because it coincides with positive results that fit the brain's expectations. However, the actual act of exercising feels bad because it goes against the brain's natural performance abilities. As you consciously act upon your expectation to exercise your performance ability will gradually increase as new circuits are wired, and the brain's negative emotions will decrease.

Any time you attempt to act or think beyond the brain's perception of your natural capacity, you will have a negative response. Any time your environment presents you with something contrary to the brain's recorded information, you will also experience a negative response.

Often our minds think, "I can't do this!" or "This is impossible!" Your brain evaluates what it knows and can do in the present moment; if you cannot do a task, the brain says, "I can't." Pay attention to the times you feel or think this way. Stop yourself and think, "But I can learn!" When something seems impossible, think, "That is only because my mind doesn't know how it can be done. But I can work to find out how to make this possible."

There Is a Positive Emotional Reaction when Stimuli Match Existing Neural Circuits

Let's say you have an inner desire to go out with a particular person. Let's name that person Jordan. If Jordan calls you, you will have a positive emotional reaction. Jordan could call someone else that doesn't know him or her, and that "someone else" would not have the same reaction as you. Jordan does not have the power to make someone feel a certain way. It is a person's internal wiring, his or her beliefs and expectations, that creates the reaction.

Positive reactions work the same as negative reactions. In this book, "negative" refers to anything that we find unpleasant; "positive," to anything we find pleasing. This next story combines positive and negative reactions.

I was told a story about a newlywed couple. The wife fixed meals with leftovers. The wife felt good about her meals because she believed her husband would be pleased to know that his wife could be creative and thrifty. The husband, unaware of her goal, felt sad because he thought someone that truly loved him would find joy in making new meals for him each day.

The point of the story is that an action can have opposing reactions, depending on the perspective of a person. The wife felt a positive reaction to her behavior. The husband had a negative emotional reaction. Remember: these perspectives are literally recorded in our brains. Some of you may read this story and wonder why the husband didn't help prepare the meal. Why did he expect the wife to fix something for him? Why didn't he love her enough to fix some of the meals? Some readers may wonder how they had the *time* to fix meals in their home. Down the road, readers may ask, "What are 'leftovers'?"

How do these expectations, hopes, perspectives, and so forth get recorded? Look back at the beginning of this book and read the section "Who Are You?" (Day 3) to see how they are developed. How are *you* feeling about this information? Do you have positive feelings? Does learning this excite you, or do you feel bored, unimpressed, or confused? All your reactions come from the expectations and understandings you have in your brain.

Keep paying attention to your thoughts, and start paying attention to your emotions.

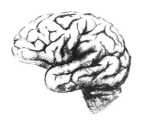

Day 15

The next points about emotions will help you find a way to influence what is recorded in your brain. As you gain further insight into your emotions, you will see why changing can be difficult, and you will learn ways to use the brain effectively for making changes.

Everything Is Relative

Keep things in perspective. The fact that everything is relative has a profound impact on how we think and feel.

In the last few days, I told you where feelings come from. Do you remember? They are reactions that your brain triggers according to what is wired in it. If something happens that stops you from getting what you want, you become sad or maybe even mad. For example, if you do poorly on a test and you expected to do well, you will be disappointed. If you get a better grade than expected, you will be happy. Your brain doesn't care what the score is; it cares only what your standard or ideal is, as well as the outcome in relation to that ideal.

What difference does this make? Who cares? This is why we should all care: the brain does not know the ideal level of work needed to be successful, the ideal level of comfort, the ideal level of money to be happy, and so on. In fact, what *is* the ideal level? What is the ideal weight, job, relationship, or strength? What is the ideal number of games to win?

Your brain would be happy with you earning $40,000 a year if you'd been homeless for most of your life. Your brain would feel happy about working only eight hours a day for the income you have if, in the past, you'd worked ten or more hours a day for the same amount. Five hours a day would feel awful if you had once been able to maintain the same living on two hours a day.

This truth awakens you to the fact that your expectations of life's events and circumstances are established by past experiences and beliefs you've developed. Your expectations, or standards, are not necessarily founded upon expert experience or research. Your brain alerts you only to differences. It has no innate capacity to make an accurate judgement. It will continue to seek to meet and exceed your own well-insulated expectations.

Compare this with climbing a mountain. You get to the top and feel great excitement. Then you look around and see higher mountains. Your friends may be on those higher mountains. Suddenly you want to be on top of the higher mountain. If you are not careful, you will constantly seek after higher mountains and not fully appreciate the mountain you are on.

You can use this knowledge to your advantage! Appreciate the progress you have made so far on a goal, or the blessings you have in life. When you feel discouraged, you can stop on your climb up the mountain and be grateful for your progress. Many social experts highly recommend, based on research, a daily moment of gratitude. I've just explained to you why this is the case. The brain will constantly push you to higher places as you reestablish your norm of expectations. You will be at risk for frequent disappointment unless you consciously decide to appreciate both your progress and your present blessings.

Finally, knowing this can help prevent regression. If you flub things or life isn't as great as you'd like, your brain will eventually accept this unfortunate situation. If something unfortunate happens again and you don't do anything about it, your brain will adjust. Soon you could find yourself way down the mountain, or perhaps in a pit. You may wonder, "What just happened?" This is what happened: you didn't notice yourself going down the hill. As your expectations and hopes slowly began to drop, so too did your behaviors. Now that you understand that your reactions and behaviors are a result of expectations in your mind, you can consciously determine your expectations and goals and not let them slip even if you fumble.

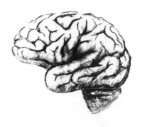

Day 16

We've been talking about emotions. By now you probably know we feel emotions because our brains react to what we experience or think about in the environment. We react negatively if a situation is against what we would expect and positively if it meets or exceeds what we would expect. These expectations are based on our experiences and not on what really is good or bad.

What happens to those emotions you feel? They fade away. This is fact 6.

Emotional Responses Fade

The fading of emotional responses is known as habituation. Understanding this is monumental for relationships, goal setting, and staying on the right track. It occurs because emotions work as an alarm system to make us aware of things in order to lead us to or from opportunities. When a threat comes, you will feel an emotion that alerts you to it. If you continue to be in the same situation or make the same choice and no bad consequence happens, you grow accustomed to the experience and the brain stops signaling you to take notice. The emotion, whether for good or bad in the long run, will fade. When a perceived good opportunity comes but does not produce the expected outcomes, the positive emotions will fade.

Think of a time when you hurt yourself physically; the pain

may have been overbearing at first. Gradually the pain subsided. When some bad things happen, we may first have overwhelmingly disappointed, angry, or depressed feelings. As time goes on, the feelings gradually lessen. Positive feelings fade too. Can you remember a time when you were excited about a new goal? How long did your excitement last?

Why Would the Brain Want Feelings to Fade?

The brain's first goal is protection. So if a stimulus appears to threaten your peace of mind or harm you, your brain will have a response appropriate for keeping you safe or happy. For example, the presence of people will at first scare deer. When, however, the deer see no real danger associated with the presence of the people, they no longer have an internal response to protect themselves by running away. Likewise, if we at first think it is wrong to do something but do not see any immediate punishment resulting from that thing (poor health due to something we eat, for example), the "shouldn't do this" feeling fades and we develop the poor habit.

The second goal of the brain is to be happy. The brain will trigger strong positive feelings about something good to do (such as starting to exercise or do better on homework). If we do not do something that elicits a reward soon enough to satisfy our expectations, this feeling will fade. This also occurs when we buy something new. At first we feel excited about it, but then the excitement fades. There is no need for the brain to motivate you to action; you already made the purchase. Have you been excited about reaching a new level on a computer game or winning a ball game? This feeling fades too. Your brain doesn't need to send constant signals that winning was good. You accomplished the task. Now it is ready for the next feel-good moment. (This is like getting to the top of a mountain, as I explained earlier.)

In summary, repeated stimuli regarding something that the brain does not see as harmful or helpful cause motivation or protection signals to fade away. You or your environment have "taught" your brain that the action is not harmful or needful (or it is already accomplished). Or, if a new habit has been developed, you have created a new neurological pathway.

For me, the facts of relativity and habituation are the most practical truths I can apply. I accept that some experiences are difficult, but I can improve the way I feel by changing my perspective regarding the circumstance. Sometimes I can be patient, knowing the bad feelings are temporary. Other times, I can feel better by focusing on the good things in my life.

You can use these facts to help you too. I hope you understand the importance of paying attention to your initial responses and know that they have the potential to fade.

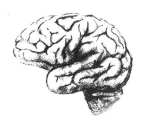

Day 17

For several days, I talked to you about our emotions. By now you may have discovered that your brain is not trying to develop the real you. It merely absorbs and responds to what is in its environment—physical or spiritual. You can be in control by taking charge of your environment. Chapter 4, starting with day 23, teaches how to take charge and make changes.

You also now know that the purpose of emotions is to move us to action and change. So what do we do when we *don't* feel excited or fearful about something? We do what is easy. This is because changing takes energy. Emotions provide the necessary energy. Without emotions, we must decide to exert the energy. That is why changing and improving are so hard. Today's reading will explain why.

The Brain Is Lazy

The brain is designed for efficiency, not to be your life coach. That is a nice way of saying that the brain is lazy. Don't be offended; this isn't about you. The *brain* is lazy. Knowing what to do is good, but it is not enough. Have you ever heard people talking about finding your why? Well, this is *why* you need to find your why.

We behave and think according to our neuron connections, neurotransmitters, and hormones. We do things that we can, want, or must do. Let me repeat that. We do things we

- can (in the case of a well-insulated neuron circuit),
- want to (when stimuli excite neurons that release chemicals that produce strong emotions or may be part of a well-insulated circuit for expectations, habits, values, or beliefs), or
- have to (when stimuli excite neurons that warn of punishment).

Bad habits are unfortunate examples. We can know something is not good for us, but the habit will win every time unless we find that we *have* to quit doing it to avoid a consequence we don't want. These circuits can be so strong sometimes that, for some people, even knowing a habit is life-threatening does not change behavior. Likewise, we can know something is good and beneficial to do (such as exercising), but until we really *want* or *have* to do it (according to the brain's processing), we won't.

Again: if we cannot do a task, we must *want to* or *have to* do it.

We usually refer to the ability to overcome bad habits or debilitating feelings as "willpower." Studies have examined the mechanisms behind this abstract term. Results indicate that the anterior cingulate cortex plays a role in helping people act in the most optimal way during tempting circumstances.

A more positive view of this fact regarding the brain is that knowing is the first step to doing. And guess what! I will later teach you how to *use* this concept to move you to action.

Think about what you do each day. What activities do you *have* to do? What do you *want* to do? Is there anything you would like to do but do not do? Why not? Think about today's topics. I really want to help you achieve lasting happiness, and that means learning to do what is not easy. I'll write more about this again so you can learn how to do the things that are not easy for you.

Stimulus ⟶ Response Chart

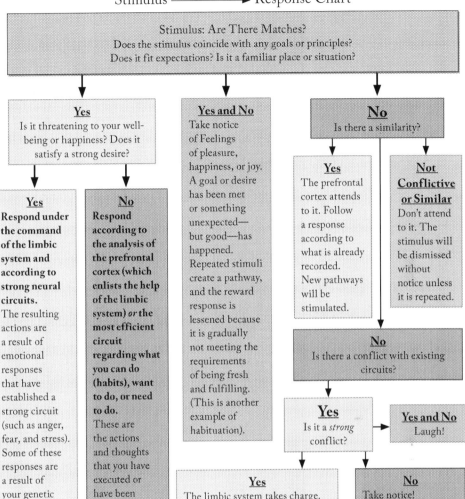

Stimulus: Are There Matches?
Does the stimulus coincide with any goals or principles?
Does it fit expectations? Is it a familiar place or situation?

Yes
Is it threatening to your well-being or happiness? Does it satisfy a strong desire?

Yes and No
Take notice of Feelings of pleasure, happiness, or joy. A goal or desire has been met or something unexpected—but good—has happened. Repeated stimuli create a pathway, and the reward response is lessened because it is gradually not meeting the requirements of being fresh and fulfilling. (This is another example of habituation).

No
Is there a similarity?

Yes
Respond under the command of the limbic system and according to strong neural circuits. The resulting actions are a result of emotional responses that have established a strong circuit (such as anger, fear, and stress). Some of these responses are a result of your genetic make-up.

No
Respond according to the analysis of the prefrontal cortex (which enlists the help of the limbic system) or the most efficient circuit regarding what you can do (habits), want to do, or need to do. These are the actions and thoughts that you have executed or have been exposed to most often.

Yes
The prefrontal cortex attends to it. Follow a response according to what is already recorded. New pathways will be stimulated.

Not Conflictive or Similar
Don't attend to it. The stimulus will be dismissed without notice unless it is repeated.

No
Is there a conflict with existing circuits?

Yes
Is it a *strong* conflict?

Yes and No
Laugh!

Yes
The limbic system takes charge. Alert for change and establish a new response circuit. Note that when the person behaves contrary to the alert, he or she will establish a circuit that will lessen the conflicting feelings if nothing bad happens as a result (habitation). However, until the new circuit is stronger than the conflicting views, there will be negative feelings (such as anger, fear, depression, shock, stress, and guilt). If the person heads the alert, the brain will make another strong alert signal again under the same circumstances, this time more quickly . If the person triggers an alert signal often, this reaction will create a well-insulated, easily-accessed pathway.

No
Take notice! Respond according to the analysis of the prefrontal cortex. There may be varying degrees of discomfort depending on the level of conflict. In this case, something is different but not emotionally significant. With repeated stimulus, it will become a match. The stimulus can eventually become easily retrievable information or a habit.

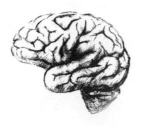

Day 18

Today is just a review day. I made a diagram to illustrate what takes place between the time of the introduction of a stimulus and the formulation of a response. All temporal signals come in through the senses. These may be exact matches with neural pathways, or they may have similarities to or contain elements that conflict with existing neural pathways. If there is a match *and* the match is well insulated and the synapse strong, the person experiencing the match will behave according to how she always behaves regarding the given stimulus. The more familiar a stimulus, the shorter the reaction time. This is what makes it possible for us to eat, talk, walk, and do all other everyday activities as efficiently as we do. If a stimulus activates several neural circuits, it will travel more quickly through the most efficient (well-insulated) one.

Most stimuli throughout the day will be a combination of those that are similar, the same, conflicting, or new. When a new stimulus excites an existing circuit, the body will take notice of it and compare it with existing connections. If a stimulus is the achievement of a goal or expectation, positive feelings are produced by the emotional center of your brain. For example, you will get excited when you finish in first place in a competition. If it is the first time you've accomplished this, you will be extremely excited. If you have won first place before, you will be happy, but not to the same degree. This is a result of habituation, as mentioned in truth 5.

In this section, I have shared facts about the brain and how it affects our behavior and feelings. These facts will aid us in achieving the goals we have.

From this information, we can conclude that there are three critical aspects for happiness:

1. Having in your brain what you *really* desire
2. Making your goals *easy* to pursue or do
3. Being able to distinguish between a true warning and a false alarm, as well as between an impulse and a good push in the right direction

Let's look at the four traits for a moment with respect to what I just shared:

Be Humble by Having an Attitude of Learning

An attitude of learning allows opportunity to discover what will really benefit you instead of relying on your brain's limited knowledge of what will bring about the best results.

Reflect upon What You Wish to Do, How You Behave, and the Reactions You Wish to Have

Because your mind assumes that what it knows is right and correct, it is important that you think about your behaviors and their effects. Are there behaviors you want to change? Is there something you need to better understand in relation to the people around you, your money-related habits, or your job?

Be Open-Minded by Listening

Because everyone is different and your own mind will not naturally see everyone's perspective, you must consciously decide to be open-minded.

Be Committed to What Is True, Be Willing to Change What Is Not, and Stay True to the Real You

Because your brain will fight against (in other words, produce negative feelings toward) anything that goes contrary to what is stored in it, you will have to be firm in your resolve to change behaviors. This will take energy.

3

Improving What Lies Within, Part 1: Understanding Change

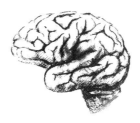

Day 19

In the previous chapter, I established what we need to do to be happy:

1. We must have in our brains what we *really* desire. (This is addressed in chapter 4.)
2. We must make our goals *easy* to pursue or achieve. (This is accomplished by applying the information in chapter 4.)
3. We must be able to distinguish between a true warning and a false alarm, and between an impulse and a good push. (This is explained in chapter 5.)

Before going on to the next chapter, I need to explain what happiness does not and cannot rely on: your environment. Nothing in the world will lay out an easy course for developing our true selves or achieving our true goals. "The good life" doesn't just present itself to anyone. In fact, we are constantly encountering problems. Problems are results of either (1) being in an imperfect world with imperfect people where both wrong intentions and mishaps happen or (2) being imperfect and acting upon incorrect beliefs, perceptions, or values that we have developed. Remember: we can behave according only to what we understand or are skilled at doing. Sometimes when we do this, we behave in ways that are counterproductive and later cause problems.

It is true that there are some people born in an environment many can only dream of—one in which tangible rewards are easy to come by. Some are part of a loving, supportive family. Others have grown up in a family with awesome possessions. Despite these advantages, no man or woman can live effortlessly. No one can assume he will obtain all that he truly desires. As a result, everyone—no matter what environment he or she is in—needs solutions to solve problems and overcome the great dilemmas or challenges threatening his or her happiness and blocking his or her road to success. If you don't fully believe this, study the life of someone famous. Performers, politicians, and business leaders have all had difficulties to overcome, and all of them have had to put in a lot of effort. Steve Jobs was even fired from the very company he helped create. Because of his attitude, this didn't ruin his career. It altered it.

We must also understand that even when a person achieves a goal, the ending is not "and she lived happily ever after." Instead it is "and she lived happily for a time period." Remember habituation? Positive emotions that come from meeting an expectation fade.

This is important to know because life will present some tough roads to travel and boulders to avoid. If a person has a belief that life should be easy, that person will often be crippled by negative emotions.

Today I pointed out that everyone has challenges in life. I also shared with you what we cannot rely upon for our happiness: the environment.

Tomorrow's topic: you and your happiness.

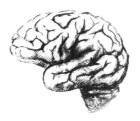

Day 20

Yesterday I closed with the idea that everyone has challenges in life. Challenges, which are circumstances that oppose our expectations, create unwanted feelings. You learned in the last chapter that this is a natural result. However, these feelings do not have to stop you! You and your goals are too important to give up on. Chapters 4, 5, and 6 will help you learn how to keep going and not give up.

Right now, I want to again review the key ideas for happiness. For us to be happy, we must

1. have in our brains what we *really* desire,
2. make our goals easy to pursue or achieve, and
3. be able to distinguish between a true warning and a false alarm.

In point 1, I state that it is essential to record in your brain what you are ultimately want. This is a simple statement that addresses the need for you to have recorded in your mind what is paramount to you instead of what the environment around you has taught you over the years. This is not to say that everything you have learned is bad. This is just to say that marketing and media can give us the wrong ideas of what would really make us happy in the long run. Happiness is not making ourselves look just like a model or otherwise look cool via the latest fashions. It is not being the smartest person in the room or the best athlete. These things make us feel good *momentarily*.

A massive number of books and articles about happiness have been written, so there is no way I can share with you all the truths that will help you be happy. I just hope that reading this book will help increase your desire to learn the truths necessary to achieve happiness.

I can't share everything about how to be happy, but I want to share some facts about happiness. Brains, as I mentioned before, want to be happy according to what is wired in them. However, happiness, or success, comes from acting upon a fixed set of principles or facts. Yes, even the little moments of positivity are a result of acting upon a fixed set of principles. Even a positive feeling that may later cause negativity is a result of acting upon a fixed set of principles or facts. For example, eating chocolates may produce a moment of relief and joy, but eating too many of them will cause a person to gain weight and will not resolve issues in one's life.

We cannot argue or change laws of nature, be they physical or social. Airplanes fly because someone designed them based on facts; they do not defy the law of gravity. The design of the aircraft took the problem of gravity into consideration. We cannot follow certain ideas and then expect a certain outcome if we do not follow the laws to obtain the outcome. Unfortunately, we may not have access to necessary truths or principles in our own mind yet. Regardless, happiness is a result of outcomes from fixed principles or facts. In fact, psychologists and scientists have found ways we can make ourselves feel better just by applying certain principles. Smiling is the best example. If you are feeling down, you can improve your mood simply by smiling. You can research smiling on the internet for details of this phenomenon.

On the other hand, let's consider the story of the Edsel, as mentioned on day 8. Positive thinking did not create ultimate happiness in this case. The designers created a car that people did not find appealing. I am certain many of them were genuinely happy as they made the plans, because in their minds they believed they were going to hit the jackpot with this new car. The short-term success or happiness they felt was based on the conclusions of the set principles in their own minds. Their plans, however, did not meet the requirement for overall success or happiness, which was to create a car that many people wanted to buy.

Think of relationships in this regard as well. You can treat a person any way you wish, but if you do not treat the person based upon what will truly create a positive relationship with *that* person, you will be rejected. It is not that there is a fixed way to treat all people. People are unique and have unique needs. However, most people generally respond favorably to several basic principles of which psychologists write and religious leaders preach.

We can choose any behavior or thought. We cannot choose the outcome. Results are based upon natural laws or truths. To get the results we want, we follow the truths that create those results.

Of course, sometimes there is more than one path to a result. For example, happiness can be derived from being with loved ones, achieving a goal, or doing an enjoyable activity. Sometimes we can follow the "rules" of paths that will later cause harm, such as partaking of substances with ingredients that affect our brains' reward systems and give immediate pleasure. The "law" of substance is that one must consume it to feel its effects. Adults can buy alcohol and store it in their houses. They can even look at it regularly. It won't have any negative effect on their brains until they consume it.

Laws, truths, and principles exist. They just do. We have different ideas about what laws and facts exist; mankind is still trying to figure them all out. However, they exist even if we don't know about them or the intricate parts of them. History is full of stories of mankind's discoveries of laws and truths. In the field of medicine, for example, when the existence and effects of germs were unknown, nurses spread illnesses throughout hospitals. Even in the twenty-first century we are learning about germs and how to prevent their spread!

Many times, mankind has been wrong. In the Middle Ages, Europeans held on to the idea the world is flat. Copernicus hypothesized that the sun was the middle of the universe instead of the earth, which seemed completely absurd to others of his time. Galileo, with the help of an avid supporter, was able to prove Copernicus's theory. In addition, archaeologists are always making new discoveries. The understanding of the brain has evolved as well. Gall believed the shape of the skull determined what was in the brain. Broca challenged Gall. When Broca studied persons with language problems, he found an area that was associated with language and not associated with the shape of the skull. He disproved Gall's theory.

Persons in sports and theatre practice the discovery of facts through trial and error. A basketball player asks himself, "What must I do to put this ball into the hoop?" An actress wonders, "How can I elicit an emotional response from the audience?" Social psychologists experiment to see what the "laws" of relationships and success are. Thought leaders use metaphors, such as bank accounts and buckets, to describe these truths. Personally, I think a great metaphor for relationships is the creation of very fragile pottery. What kind of metaphor would you use to explain the truths about relationships? What have you learned?

I don't know all the laws relating to success and happiness. I'm simply stating that they exist, and it is important for you to understand that they exist. Motivational speakers and psychologists refer to this as mindset. Long-term happiness comes from acting upon true principles and laws of social science, or a healthy mindset.

No matter what the ability of one's brain is, based on its physical functioning capacities, we must seek to do the things that will naturally produce happiness. Sometimes we are wrong about what will bring us happiness. This book's information is meant to help you find lasting happiness *sooner*, and perhaps less painfully.

You made it to day 20!

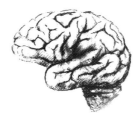

Day 21

Let's look at our list of what it takes to be happy.

1. We must have in our brains what we are *really* desire.
2. We must make our goals easy to pursue or do.
3. We must distinguish between a true warning and a false alarm.

It's time to start taking the steps toward getting what it takes to be happy! Tomorrow we'll talk about the first "must" of improvement. Take the time to think about what you've learned so far about happiness. In preparation for improving your life, think about what you hope to see improved.

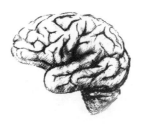

Day 22

We want to figure out what we truly want to be, become, and think so the brain is equipped with our real goals and what is really rewarding to us. This is a continual process; we will always be learning what our true selves are. It will take a lifetime of learning to understand truth and to act upon it. Remember: truth exists. Facts exist. We simply don't know all the facts and skills to act upon them. That is why it is important to want to keep learning. Previously I called truths the laws of social science. According to many, these are truths of a supreme being, higher power, or the universe.

Make a list of what you want to be and what you want to become or accomplish in life. This is, most likely, a list of who you really are and what you are truly after. After you've made your list, look at your goals. What is it about your goals that has made you want to pursue them? To understand the question I'm asking, let's look at a basketball game. Winning is based on a fixed law: the team to get the most balls through the hoop wins. Therefore, team members must build the skill to accurately aim for the hoop. Thus, the goal is to be good at aiming for the hoop. But why? Because winning feels good. Playing the game feels good, and winning feels even better. Everyone chooses to pursue something that makes them feel satisfaction. We may have different goals, but the reasons for our goals are always the same. Whatever your desire, it brings happiness. As you work toward finding out who you really are and what you really want, it is important to understand why you pursue what you pursue.

Because it is happiness and peace that you really want, the real you seeks for that happiness and peace in behavior, thought, and goal setting.

After you have had some time to think about what you really want, it is time to ask another critical question: "How do I *know* that what I am doing will truly bring me satisfaction in the end?"

You may end up changing some behaviors when you realize that the behaviors will not ultimately give you what you want.

Other questions to ask are as follows:

- What actions does my mind want to do that will not bring satisfaction in the end? (Consider actions [usually poor habits] that you do because you feel compelled to do them.)
- As I've grown up, what has my brain learned that really isn't true? (These are beliefs that will stop us from pursuing the real goals we want to achieve.

It is because of the unhelpful "goals" and beliefs of our minds that we need to regularly evaluate goals, habits, lifestyles, and daily choices. In other words, we must continually consider who we really are and what we really want. After all, our own understanding is limited.

We must be convinced that what we choose to do or pursue is really what we want. Initially, the goals that require you to make changes will produce negative feelings because the goals will not be as familiar or easy as the unhealthy "goals" your brain is already working on.

Remember the following:

- We do the easiest and most familiar things we are literally wired to do.
- We are biologically wired to feel satisfaction regarding what is wired, not necessarily regarding what is best.

Because of the above, please keep the following in mind:

- We need to wire our new goals in our minds so that they will be easy, familiar, and satisfactory.
- We need to wire our new goals in our minds so that they will be easy, familiar, and satisfactory.
- We need to wire our new goals in our minds so that they will be easy, familiar, and satisfactory.

Why do we need to wire new goals? So these goals will be easy, familiar, and satisfactory. Wiring the new goals (and truths) in our minds will make them easy to pursue. I'll take several days to explain how to upgrade your brain's wiring.

Improving What Lies Within, Part 2: Upgrading the Brain's Wiring

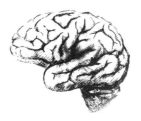

Day 23

It will take a few days to explain how to upgrade the brain's wiring because there are two steps to this procedure. The first step is explained on days 23–26. The second step, briefly mentioned on day 27, is so involved that it takes fourteen days, an entirely new chapter, to explain.

At this point you have read about what it means to biologically record something. For this to happen, our senses must receive the same signal frequently, or a signal must produce strong emotions. Strong emotions motivate the body toward action. Motivational speakers do a great job of appealing to the emotions. This is not bad, but people can mistakenly believe that a strong emotional experience is all they need to change. Instead, recorded information and skills help us *do* the actions. It is important to have the right recordings, as they are what our brains use to behave, think, and feel.

Upgrading your brain is all about developing and strengthening the types of beliefs, principles, expectations, habits, traits, goals, and values that will bring you the most productive behaviors in this life. This book does not share all truths and essential values for you. That is not possible or practical. Instead you will learn how to discover them and how to wire them.

The first task in upgrading your brain is to install the four traits mentioned at the beginning of this course. To install the traits, we must consciously choose them.

1. Choose to have an attitude of learning and to be open-minded.
2. Choose to be reflective by thinking twice.
3. Choose to build a smart brain by being open-minded and willing to change.
4. Choose to have ultimate satisfaction and you will stay true to the real you.

Choose to Have an Attitude of Learning and to be Open-Minded.

Because we act upon what we have stored in our minds, one of the simplest commitments we can make is to keep learning. The more we learn and understand the importance of something, the stronger our desire to do it will become. The more we understand the harm of something, the harder it will be to do it. Be smart; don't leave your knowledge to chance. Continue to be active in learning.

- Want to increase your likelihood for work opportunities? Learn as much as you can about your career interests and self-improvement.
- Want to improve relationships? Learn about what the important people in your life are interested in. Learn about activities and services you can do for them.
- Want to stop a habit? Learn about the harms of it, how others have overcome it, and which habits you can replace it with. Do not rely on your own knowledge or skills. Increase your knowledge by learning from others or from appropriate media sources or books.

I know this seems so simplistic, but this step is important. The brain produces thoughts and behaviors according to what is in it, whether we put it in there (by reading, watching, listening) or someone else puts it in there (our environment, which we don't control). In other words, if you don't seek to learn and improve your knowledge and skills, the only option you have for improvement is to wait for someone or something to help you.

Not only is it important to be proactive in what you are learning, but you will also want to examine what your environment is now teaching you. Your teaching environment consists of people and organizations in your life and the media you view (internet, TV, movies, newspapers, magazines, etc.). Examine yours for a moment.

You are not always in control of what people around you may say or do. You can, however, counteract this influence by what you choose to read and watch. At this time, you may not even need to change or improve anything in your environment. If you are happy with the way things are, stay in control to keep it that way.

What if you aren't happy and you don't think you can do anything to change your situation? You may be thinking of a lot of problems that prevent you from changing your environment. You may wonder what you can do to influence your mind for good. Read uplifting books or watch uplifting videos. In the beginning of this book I mentioned I know most circumstances are too complex to fix simply by reading a book. The key point is that this information can change what is in your mind slightly to start you on a path toward finding the answers to your complex situation. The first step toward change is changing what is in your mind. This book presents some ideas for your mind to think about. From here you may get ideas to do something that will start you on a path to an improved life.

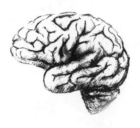

Day 24

Yesterday I shared with you the first trait to install for improving your life. Do you remember what that first attitude is? It is the attitude to keep learning. Today I'll explain about the second trait to install.

Choose to Think Twice and Be Reflective.

Thinking twice before you make a decision or do something gives your working memory a chance to sort through all the information it has recorded. Initial reactions come from the most insulated or emotional circuits. Some of the information recorded in your mind, information that could be very helpful, is recorded on very fragile and weak connections; these can be easily neglected. Slow down. Be who you really are, not what the outside world has driven you to be. Value what is really of worth to you, not what marketing strategies claim you should value.

Thinking twice can help us when we believe a situation is hopeless. For example, when a student of mine messes up on an art project or writing attempt, often the child feels upset and exclaims, "I can never do this!" or "I'm terrible." I teach these students to think twice and react differently. I teach them to see that they are just learning to write and draw. I teach them to say, "I didn't do that right. I can try again and get better."

Sometimes I feel discouraged when I don't accomplish something as I initially had hoped. I, too, have to think twice and decide not to give up. Sometimes a person may do something I don't think is right; when I think twice about the situation, sometimes I realize I don't have all the information. Other times, others don't have all the information.

Think twice about what you pursue (intentionally or unintentionally). Think twice about what you say and do. Use your mind, your prefrontal cortex, and your working memory. Your brain assumes that your perspective is correct and normal. This isn't a bad feature of the brain; we just need to make certain that what we become is true to ourselves and congruent with truth. This step is very helpful as you interact with others. Think twice before you react; think twice about your perspective, and think twice about your opinion. You don't know everything. You don't know the circumstances of those around you; nor do you know what is in their minds. Choose to think twice. Challenge your own thinking and behavior.

Thinking twice does not mean your initial reaction is always wrong. Rather, it is an opportunity to catch yourself in the times when you want to act differently from your initial reaction. The intent is not to always second-guess yourself. In fact, the more you can record in your mind the behaviors and thoughts of your true self, the more your first reactions will be aligned with what you truly want. Thinking twice trains your mind to access as much information as possible.

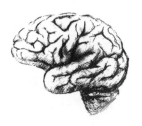

Day 25

Today I get to share with you the third trait for upgrading the wiring of the brain. Close your eyes for a moment and think of the actions for installing the first two traits. Continue reading after you have a guess.

Did you think of "choose to keep learning" and "choose to think twice and reflect often"? More importantly, have you taken these actions?

Choose to Build a Smart Brain by Being Open-Minded and Willing to Change

Choosing to be smarter than the brain is important for two reasons. We have incorrect information that will create strong negative feelings (to stop you) and "pushings" (positive feelings that motivate us to do something) that will not be beneficial in the end. Sometimes these feelings can be so strong that, unless we consciously choose otherwise, they will win every time. The very purpose of emotion is to motivate us. We cannot overpower these mechanisms unless we have *decided* that we are going to do something contrary to what we have been programmed to do. We decide to go contrary to programming when we have some knowledge that the feelings we have (negative or positive) will not bring real satisfaction in the end.

Let me restate a key sentence: we cannot overpower these mechanisms (strong emotions) unless we have decided that we are going to do something contrary to what we have been programmed to do. Why would we want to do this? Because we have some knowledge that the feelings we have, whether negative or positive, will not bring real satisfaction in the end.

Going against emotions is the journey across a bridge of life that can make you feel as if you are on green ground, crossing over to dry fields—or maybe from dry ground to a forest fire. It is a feeling of safety only because where you are now is familiar and easy. However, once you begin to cross to the other side (ignore your emotions and do what you know is best), you will begin to realize you were on dry ground or in a forest fire all along! You may also describe this feeling of changing as an uphill climb.

Remember these implications about the brain:

- The brain assumes that what it knows is right.
- The brain has a negative reaction to anything that conflicts with it. This could take the form of anger, disappointment, fear, jealousy, doubt, etc. The brain warns us wrongfully with thoughts such as "not possible," "wrong," "stupid," and "awful." Because of these reactions, you will have to choose to ignore these messages and do what you have decided is correct to say, do, feel, or think. Eventually you will find out what is on the other side of your present thinking.

At this moment, you are living a particular life and feel a particular way based on the present recordings in your brain. When you act contrary to these recordings, you will have a negative reaction. When you have an opportunity that enhances these beliefs, you will feel a surge of positive feelings.

When you ignore the negative (or hyperpositive and distracting) feelings and choose to add new recordings, you will have new information for your brain to analyze. Let's look at that again: As soon as you ignore the negative (or hyperpositive but distracting) feelings you have (in other words, when you choose to be smarter than the brain) and add new recordings (by learning new ideas, thinking new thoughts, or doing something different), you will have new information to analyze.

It is exciting to find out what experiences and feelings your new reactions create. You will be on the other side of negative fears or doubts. Thinking twice gives you the opportunity to consider the other side. Being smarter than your brain gives you the power to follow through with a different thought or behavior. But remember that thinking twice and being smarter than the brain does not mean you must always act contrary to your initial reaction; rather, doing these things will provide you with the opportunity to catch yourself during the times when you *want* to act differently from your initial reaction. Taking these actions will allow you to develop the power to do what you know is best.

It will take several moments of overcoming your brain's control before you see the fruits of your labor, so the final choice—to desire ultimate satisfaction—is important.

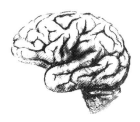

Day 26

Today I will share the fourth and final part of upgrading the wiring in your brain. But first, as you may guess, I want you to try to think of what the other three parts are. This time I'm not going to write them here for you. I want you to have the opportunity to really check your understanding. Go back to day 23 and check your answer. (Can you tell I'm a teacher?)

Choose to Have Ultimate Satisfaction, and You Will Stay True to the Real You

Have there been days when you haven't wanted to do something but you did it anyway? For example, perhaps you did not want to get out of bed one morning. Why did you do what you didn't really want to do? Staying in bed would've been an immediate reward, but there was an ultimate reward you wanted. Can you see that without the desire for ultimate satisfaction, we are left at the mercy of what our brains believe is most beneficial for us at the moment? Ultimate satisfaction isn't about being deprived, though your brain might tell you that. Choosing ultimate satisfaction is postponing your reward. Eventually you will no longer need will power to carry out your actions for what you ultimately want. You will have finally weeded out the circuit that *desired* the immediate satisfaction as well as the *responses* that produced the immediate satisfaction.

To aid yourself in choosing ultimate satisfaction, identify the actions or words that you do, say, or think that you wish to eliminate. These are actions and words that bring some sense of satisfaction at a given moment. Perhaps these include the habit of smoking, eating certain types (or amounts) of foods, or interacting with people in negative ways. After identifying the behavior you want to change, discover the reasons for wanting to eliminate it. Think of as many reasons as you can. Write down or memorize these reasons. These are your ultimate rewards. Think about these often—very often.

Do the same for actions that you want to begin or increase that may be difficult, or for a goal you want to achieve. Why do you want to start the new habit or achieve the goal? This is your ultimate satisfaction.

If you want to prevent problems that come from poor choices, do the same exercise. Think of why you want to change your pattern of behavior.

Keep ultimate satisfaction in mind as you consider your finances, your relationships, your health, your job, and your interests.

Don't let society (anyone or anything) rob you of your ultimate rewards and feelings of accomplishment. You do not have to react negatively to people that may discourage you, but you can remain steadfast by keeping your eye on the real goal. And *please* don't let your own brain rob you of your ultimate rewards and feelings of accomplishment!

When you choose to have ultimate satisfaction, you don't let anyone or anything distract or discourage you.

By now you know that sometimes simply knowing and wanting is not enough—especially when choices conflict with habits that have a strong recording in your brain.

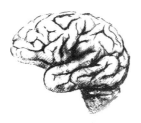

Day 27

Today we prepare to transition to a new chapter and complete the second task for upgrading the wiring in your brain. The first task was to install four traits. Do you remember the steps for doing this? (They were first introduced on day 23.) The second task is necessary because we don't remember everything we want and need to do.

The Second Task for Upgrading Is to Do a Brain Transplant

We are going to replace your brain with a new paper one. You will make decisions based upon this paper brain until your own biological brain has adapted itself to it. You can adapt it to meet your needs, but some version of this task is a must. No one's brain is perfect. We behave in ways contrary to what we really want. If what you really want to value and do is not on paper for you to review, you will rely on the biology of your brain—and I've already explained (over and over!) what that can do. The brain will push and pull you to act, think, and feel what has been well recorded by emotions and repetitive performance.

The next chapter will help you design your new brain for you to transplant. Making a paper brain is a huge task; creating the brain is almost a book in itself!

What Is a Paper Brain?

With questions and directions, I will help you write the actions you want to take to achieve your hopes. You will review this regularly (every hour, if necessary) to keep with your plans. You will stop making decisions according to what you immediately think or feel. Rather, you will make them based upon the statements and plans you have written; this is what I call your paper brain. Using it daily is the process of implanting it.

Because our brains send signals for negative emotions when we go against what we feel is true, it is helpful for us to decide what is necessary to be disappointed about and what isn't that important. For example, your body will not let you go without food, water, or sleep. You are driven to consume food and water, and your body will eventually shut itself down to sleep. These three needs are of highest priority to the brain; without them we would die.

The exercise of creating a paper brain will provide you the opportunity to prioritize your life; as a result, you can be "pushed" to do what is most critical and willing to "let go" of unimportant matters.

What Does the Paper Brain Look Like?

The paper brain involves several circles within one another. The innermost circle represents the most critical thoughts and actions for you to take. Each circle extending from it represents goals and actions of lesser importance.

The Paper Brain

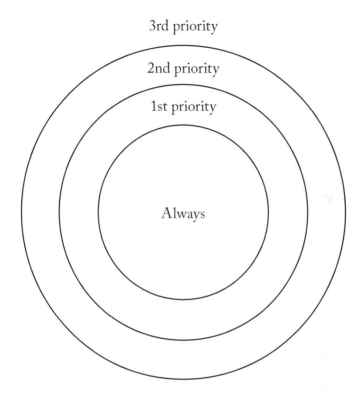

3rd priority

2nd priority

1st priority

Always

How Does the Paper Brain Work?

Because our brains adjust to the environment and pursue goals based on what is recorded in them, this process internalizes the behaviors and thoughts that are most beneficial. Differentiating the importance levels of various goals or actions with the multiple circles is essential for two reasons. Firstly, having multiple layers of priorities provides a practical plan for improvement, allowing you to work on what is most critical first. You will not be able to incorporate all the actions or goals at once. Secondly, it serves as a guide for decision-making; the items of the inner circles have greater priority.

Eventually the items listed in the paper brain will be internalized and you can adjust the paper brain with new goals.

Nobody is perfect. Nobody's life is perfect. But can we improve ourselves? Can we have peace amid an imperfect life? Can we improve our lives? I believe the answers to these questions are all yes. And that is why I use a paper brain.

5

Improving What Lies Within: Creating the Paper Brain

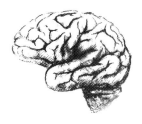

Day 28

Here is a list of the procedures for implanting a new brain.

- today: presurgery reflections
- day 31: creating your new brain
- day 39: surgery: the process of implanting your new brain
- day 41: postsurgery discussion of concerns you may have

Presurgery Preparations

So far in this book I've encouraged you to adopt or become more mindful of four specific traits. In the last chapter, I encouraged you to instill these in your mind. Now I am asking you to create a paper brain. Whatever for?

In the book's introduction is my purpose in writing this book. My purpose and hope is that you, the reader, will not be programmed by the world around you. Rather, I hope you can increase in maturity without having to go through the pains typically associated with growing up and learning.

That is my purpose for *writing* this. What is your purpose for *reading* it? What do you hope it will help you accomplish? Maybe you don't have a specific purpose in mind. Perhaps you are just reading this because you were curious or were told to. Whether you have a specific goal in mind or not, the basic goal of everyone is to decrease uncomfortable feelings and increase in satisfying feelings.

Why is this important to talk about? Preparing a paper brain is a very involved task. Unless you have a purpose and believe in that purpose, you won't want to take the steps necessary to prepare the brain. You won't have the time or energy. In addition, when you do create the paper brain, you will need to stay committed to your purpose in order to actually use the paper brain as a guide. That is the process of implanting your new brain.

Over the years, your brain has changed little by little. It is time now to take control of those changes and create the brain—the life—you want. So I ask again, what is it that you hope will happen? This will be your motivation.

At first, just make a simple statement: With a new brain, I want to be able to ...

_____.

Now take as much time as is needed to expand on the statement you wrote above.

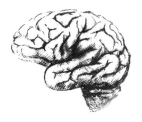

Day 29

Yesterday I told you to dream about what you would like your life to be like. Today I want to address a question you may have asked or may ask in the future: "Is there hope?"

Everyone that seems to be coasting happily down a hill of life had a climb up we didn't see. The truth is, (continuing with the metaphor), some are born with strong muscles to tolerate the climb, and some have the knowledge and skills needed to make a car and drive up. The good news is that, regardless of your climbing skills (your "grit") or knowledge, as long as you are willing to make the climb, you can be happy.

"Me?" you might ask. Yes, you. Even if you feel your situation is uncommonly—and even wrongfully—hard, there is hope for your life.

How can I make such a bold statement, considering I don't even know you?

1. I know there are a lot of organizations in existence to help people.
2. I know there a lot of men and women that have overcome great challenges and written outstanding books of hope, wisdom, and love for those circumstances.
3. I know how the mind works.

So yes, if you have desires to start (or continue) having hope for a better life and wonder if it is worth it, yes, it is. There is hope ahead. If you are tired of being in a pit and willing and ready to start climbing, yes, there is hope. You may tire of climbing. Actually, we all tire of climbing. To help you on your climb, the immune system for the soul (covered on day 43) will give you strength. First I will show you how to make a paper brain so you know what steps to take in your climb.

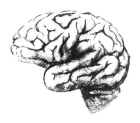

Day 30

Remember: in the beginning I told you that our brains are set up to

1. move us toward rewards (such as the wants marketed in our society);
2. protect us, producing feelings of anger and fear, which can result in a fight-or-flight response; and
3. respond quickly and as easily as possible using information gathered through life's experiences.

I also told you that the brain isn't very smart. It can analyze only what is within it. It doesn't know all facts or how others feel or think. So if you have certain dreams in your life, you will want to continually set goals. As pointed out on day 6, you will also want to read, talk, and think about things that help you achieve what you want to achieve or be like. Take charge of your thoughts because the brain isn't very reliable.

Tomorrow we will get to work and set goals to read, talk, and think about things that help you achieve what you want to achieve or be like.

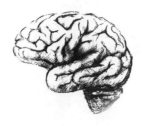

Day 31

Everything you do—I repeat, *everything* you do—is based on the brain's understanding of what is most important or normal in each given moment. With your new brain, you will define what is most important and establish actions to become your new normal. This is not to say everything you have done or will do is wrong. This is to say you are simply human and you are learning a way to improve yourself. Let's get started!

Creating the New Brain to Be Implanted

The first step of creating a paper brain is to consider all the things that are most important to you. I'm going to ask you several questions that will help you explore what is most important. Use a notebook to answer these. Don't just make this a wish list; include things you are already doing or pursuing.

Of paramount importance to the brain is survival. The first thing you must do is look at goals for your health.

Question 1: How do you want to maintain good health?

1a. What eating and exercising habits would you like to continue or start?
1b. What activities do you wish to do on a regular basis to maintain a healthy mind? These may include regular prayer or meditation.

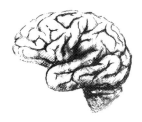

Day 32

Before you tackle another part of your brain, review yesterday's questions and answers. Do you wish to change or add to them?

Two high priorities of your brain are physical and social safety. Belonging is essential. Establish in your mind what that looks like.

Question 2: How do you want to maintain healthy relationships?

2a. With whom do you want to connect?
2b. For each of the relationships you wish to develop or maintain, write the name(s) of the person(s) most important at the top.
2c. For each name, what can you do each day, week, or month to build this relationship? You do not have to do something each day for each relationship, of course. Consider what frequency you feel is necessary to build the relationship.
2d. What memories do you want to create?
2e. What traditions do you want to establish?

Write the activities you wish to do in your notebook.

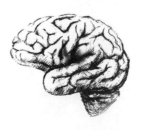

Day 33

Again, review your work so far and then consider the next part.
Another priority is feeling capable and respected.

<u>Question 3: What talents or skills do you want to share with your community or the world?</u>

    3a. What do you hope to have completed or to be doing on a regular basis when you are twenty, thirty, forty, fifty, and so on? Consider skills, activities, and achievements.

    3b. What present activities do you wish to continue? Consider your involvements in your community or school.

<u>Question 4. What activities must you do to maintain day-to-day living as you pursue your dreams?</u>

As a teenager, these activities may include cleaning your room, doing chores, completing school assignments, or practicing a skill. For an adult, these include cleaning, paying bills, performing house maintenance, getting haircuts, shopping, and so forth.

Question 5: What do you want to learn more about?

Consider your dreams; what do you need to learn more about or develop to accomplish your goal? This list, of course, won't be complete. Write down what you now realize you need to learn more about.

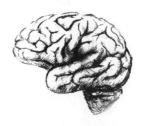

Day 34

Are you ready for the next step?

The second step for making your brain is to consider the details of your priorities: when will you perform activities? For how long will you perform them, and how often? Review your list. Add specific details.

- How frequently will you do the activities with your family or friends?
- How frequently will you do things to maintain your spirituality (connection with a higher power) or to eliminate unnecessary stress?
- How often do you want to be involved in learning (reading, watching videos, or practicing)?

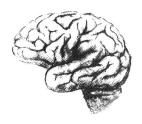

Day 35

You are getting closer to putting your brain together! For the next three days, you will prioritize your desires because you will not be able to start everything immediately. Also, from day to day, you will have issues with time. Setting priorities now is important so that you are ready to make the decisions that will help you in the long run.

Look at your lists. What are the tasks that are critical for you? What are the most important items to do? What do you feel is the bare minimum for your true self? Take your time to discover what is important for you to consistently do. In fact, this whole process may take several days. The most important tasks do not all come from the first group of questions. More than likely, you will have one or two from each group. In my case, I chose tasks that keep me focused on Christ and building relationships with my family.

Highlight these with a particular color for the inner circle.

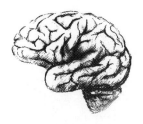

Day 36

Today we will examine another layer of priorities. What are your top priorities? Decide for yourself what your top priorities are, but choose them thoughtfully. You are activating some new circuits as you create this brain design. You have lots of time to use your working memory, so use it well.

Highlight these with a particular color for level 1.

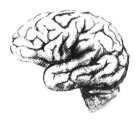

Day 37

Today is the third day for creating priorities. Which actions on the list are very important right now? Remember to be specific as you write them on your paper brain. Write specific tasks. Highlight them with a particular color for the level 2 circle.

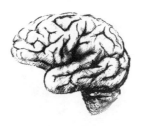

Day 38

Today is the day you get to start making your brain! The inner circle is for all the things that are musts. No ordinary excuses allowed. (Consider the actions you highlighted on day 35) The next circle is for all the actions of high priority when decision making. (Consider what you highlighted on day 36). The third layer lists important things. The outer area is a list of very good things to do in your life.

First, write all the actions you currently do in the appropriate level. Next, select actions from the questions of days 31–37. Most likely you've written or highlighted more actions than you can realistically do in your life right now because of time or resources. Choose two or three items you wish to start working on. Remember to write what they are, when you wish to do them, and how long you wish to do them.

As you incorporate the new goals into your life, you can add more goals. My brains have changed throughout the years—both the physical one and the paper one!

You did it! You just created a new brain.

By creating the paper model, you have taken the first step toward recording the types of behaviors and thoughts that will bring you the greatest sense of satisfaction. Continue to learn so you can discover the principles, values, and goals that bring you the greatest sense of satisfaction. Thinking twice will help you be the true self you are developing within.

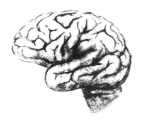

Day 39

You made your paper brain. Now it is time for surgery—time to do a brain transplant.

- Each day for thirty days, read and reflect upon your paper brain. Refine it. Think twice and keep learning during this process. Make your brain what you really want it to be. After thirty days, you should have it memorized. Reflect on it each day for a week without looking at it. If you find that you are not acting in accordance with your paper design, go back to looking at it each day. Otherwise, begin reviewing it once a week. This will give you an opportunity to evaluate what is going on and learn from your mistakes.
- Each day, act upon your paper brain.
- Use your paper brain to make a to-do list for the week or day.
- Use your paper brain to make a schedule of habits you want to begin and continue. For example, determine what you intend to do each Sunday, each morning, each evening, each Friday, each Saturday, once a month on Monday, and so on.

When reflecting, use this brain model to evaluate options. Make sure that you are not taking time, energy, or money away from something of great value. In general, you will want to make certain that you have taken care of or have scheduled everything in the two smaller circles (higher priorities) before doing anything relating to the lower priorities. As a personal example, if I really want to finish a work task relating to home or employment (an immediate reward) but I need to do something to help my son (an ultimate reward), I will spend time with my son and find time later for the work task. It may mean not getting the task done well or as soon as I'd like, but my son is more important.

In times of reflection, I consider my choices throughout the week and make changes to my paper brain as needed. There will be times when I make a wrong choice or slip up. I consider why I'm not following the paper brain plans and think of ways to make the paper brain work. Learning and being open-minded are important for effective reflection time.

During moments of decision-making, don't accept excuses from your biological brain. Be the boss. Build a smart brain. Don't listen to negative feelings or be distracted by positive pushes in other directions. Take note of these feelings and think about them when you have time to use your prefrontal cortex.

Your biological brain analyzes everything you need to do and makes decisions based on ease and reward. You are going to train your brain so that what is most important for you is easy. And because those things are important to you, they will be—albeit eventually—rewarding. Stick to your paper brain (stay committed to the true you), and your biological brain will eventually see the rewards and be on your side. Your brain can be your best friend when it has the right information recorded in it. It pushes you to do what it knows is rewarding and will create pathways for you to make the process easy. What more could you ask for?

Eventually your real brain will match what you have on paper. In other words, your natural behavior will automatically be consistent with the items you have chosen to incorporate in your life. Continually update your paper brain to keep your biological one on track.

As you become naturally inclined to do what is on your brain design, look at your original list. When appropriate, add to your paper brain. Also determine whether there any actions you would like to add to your wish list.

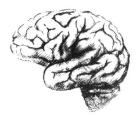

Day 40

Today I want to talk about some concerns you may have.

Q: What if time just doesn't allow me to do everything important?

A: That is why using a paper brain is so critical. We don't have time for everything. Your brain picks what it thinks is most important. The paper brain helps you take control so you can do what really *is* most important. Of course, you will have to refine your paper brain as you learn more about what really is most important.

Many companies have created equivalents to this paper brain, such as the classic Franklin Planner. Writing things down and prioritizing is not new. The paper brain is a starting point and provides an easy visual for decision-making. The *outcome* of the process is very similar to Stephen R. Covey's Quadrant II in his book *The 7 Habits of Highly Effective People.*

There will be many occasions when you will not have time to do what apparently needs to be done in your life *and* what your paper brain says should be done. Notice that I use the adverb "apparently." In other words, you are in a process of learning what is most important and needful and recognizing what just appears to be important. These frustrating moments of time conflicts can become very rewarding, victorious moments. Be true to your true self. I know it is much easier said than done, but you will be so glad you chose to build a smart brain.

The reason most of us do things that are not "best" is usually due to a less important habit or trait recorded on a strong circuit. To weaken a circuit, remember, you must not use it. It can be very difficult to ignore or eliminate something that is a significant part of you. Below are ideas to help you:

- Strengthen the new desire as much as you can; think about your goal often (or of the people it relates to). Visualize yourself executing the goal. Think about the relief and joy you will feel.
- Make a challenge of it. Decide to keep trying. When your mind decides it has to, wants to, or can do something, it will find a way to make it happen. Read day 67, which is about breaking habits if poor habits interfere with new choices you wish to make.
- Build an immune system for the soul to help with the disappointing feelings that come from not doing everything. (You can read about this in the next section of the book.)

Q: What if there is a conflict of time between things on the same priority level?

First notice that this question is about conflict regarding time or a resource of the same level. When something of truly less value conflicts with something of a high priority, we know to choose the higher priority. But what if you have a dilemma with two actions of equal priority?

A: It is not a matter of *if* this will happen, but *when*. Life is not made up of simple decisions. As we strive to create a smart brain, real conflicts of time, money, and attention arise. Life is complex, and our brains want to take the easiest route possible. Therefore, the brain often puts things that are, in the end, of little importance before things that are of great importance.

As you work toward taking control of your life (the ways you spend your time and money, and even the things you allow yourself to think about), you will learn strategies for determining what to do in times of conflict.

Consider these questions to ask yourself when conflicts regarding tasks in the same level occur:

- What will be the benefit of buying / spending the time for _____ over _____?
- At age ninety, what will I be glad I did?
- Who will be affected? What is the significance?
- What will matter the most in the long run?

This dilemma is one reason why personal mission statements have become popular. Mission statements, like the paper brain, act as a guide in making decisions. The paper brain provides your mind with specific actions and behaviors you want to do and (as mentioned earlier) is visually helpful.

Let's face it; we aren't going to make the best decisions 100 percent of the time. In fact, sometimes it will not matter. This brain model helps us make better decisions, not 100 percent perfect ones.

6

Stopping the Lies from Stopping
What Lies Within:
The Immune System for the Soul[11]

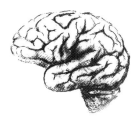

Day 41

Remember to read your brain today! Your brain is in control of what you feel in the area of your heart. Usually we react to things based on how we feel. This section will help you be in control of what you feel in your heart. Beginning on day 44, you will learn how to create an emotional immune system.

Speaking of emotions, let's first talk about how you are feeling and why. Back on day 27, I invited you to write about what you hope. Doing that activity gave you a moment to think about how you feel about your life.

Look at your answers about what you hope for someday (from days 5 and 27), and divide them up.

You		Others		Life events
what you want to do or feel	what you want to stop doing or feeling	what you hope others do.	what you want others to stop doing.	what you wish would happen for your benefit what you want changed or eliminated from your life

Your emotions, believe it or not, are meant to be helpful to you. Emotions alert you to a problem or something wonderful. They motivate you to stay away from negative situations or push you to positive ones. The list you made indicates what you want to get or get rid of.

You don't want to completely get rid of feeling bad; for example, you don't want to feel happy about falling and cutting yourself. You want to fix your body. You feel physical pain so that you will be motivated to fix whatever is wrong. You feel emotional pain to fix problems, too.

Look at your list of what you want changed. Maybe some of the things you want changed will take a while. Maybe you don't know what to do about it. You may know that you want to change you or your life, but each and every day, your heart feels heavy because you feel stuck. This is one reason why a good emotional immune system is necessary.

The paper brain will help your mind focus on the things you *can* change. Gradually, the new habits you develop can improve your life. Still, this takes time. Besides, your efforts may not immediately eliminate some of the bad things that are happening in your life. The emotional immune system will help your heart feel better as you try to figure out what you can do.

What if you don't have a lot of challenges in your life to fix? You are still at risk of becoming discouraged. Let's look at why this is.

Your Brain Is Always Seeking a Reward

Your brain always looks for better than what you now have. If you don't get your reward soon enough, your brain will trigger negative emotions.

Therefore, a healthy emotional immune system will help you feel better as you improve your life. Remember: you have little control over what others choose to do or what opportunities will come your way. This is all about taking control of what you can change. I'm not saying that it is okay for others to treat you poorly. I'm not saying that you should just shrug off the bad things that happen. I am only acknowledging the fact that we can control only our own behavior. This can affect someone else's behavior and lead to good opportunities in our lives. In the meantime, we can choose to protect ourselves from bad influences.

I hope you are not in a bad situation. I hope you don't feel absolutely hopeless. But if you do, this immune system is here to help you. I've used this immune system a lot and want to share it with others. I know that life is tough and complicated. (That is an understatement, for sure.) I don't want you to remain feeling as you do.

"Why?" you may ask. "What does it matter to you?"

I know what unhappiness feels like, to a small degree, and I don't want anyone else to feel that way. I hate knowing that the degree of unhappiness I have felt is only small compared to the degree of unhappiness many face because of hunger, loneliness, abuse, sorrow for mistakes, hardships, and difficult situations, and the list goes on.

Your situation is most likely critical and complex. To make matters worse, your mind may feed you some lies. You may think, "I am worthless" or, "It doesn't matter; there is nothing I can do. I'm stuck." Perhaps you are thinking, "I'm just not good at anything." Lies. Lies. Lies.

How, you may wonder, do I know they are lies when I don't know you or your circumstances? I'm glad you asked. (Okay, so maybe you didn't ask!)

I know that feelings of worthlessness are lies for two reasons:

1. Brain research convinces me that these thoughts are mere reactions to the faulty brain systems we have.
2. My firm belief in a supreme being leaves no question in my mind that feelings of worthlessness are absolutely not true.

Yes, you may have done things that are not good—horrible even. Yes, you may have habits that are ugly. This book isn't about learning to accept your poor traits and move on. It is about finding who you really are deep inside and becoming that person (again). It is about staying true to your true self.

If you want goodness, there is hope. You are of worth. If you don't believe me, think of this as an experiment. Test this. Whether it worked or not, contact me and share what happened. I want to know how I can better help others.

If you do feel hopeful that things will work out, you've got a great internal emotional immune system. This section will provide more ideas to boost your spirits in difficult moments. If you feel stuck, the immune system will help you get going again.

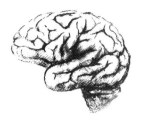

Day 42

Remember to read your paper brain!

Yesterday I told you I why I wanted to write this book; I wanted to help others that may be struggling. I learned about the body's immune system at WVU–P. I thought it would be great if we all had an immune system for the soul. I hypothesized that with an emotional immune system, we could better weather the hardships of life.

To make a long science lecture short, we have an incredible system built into our bodies to protect them from illness and disease. If we take care of our bodies, they will take care of us. In fact, we are constantly in contact with things that make us ill. Have you ever googled "germiest places"? Germs are everywhere. Because of the immune system, we often don't realize this; we continue on, feeling fine. Sometimes we do notice. When your nose runs or you cough, this is your immune system doing its job to get germs out.

If, however, the germs we encounter are too much for our external barriers and other preventative agents, our immune systems have a plan of attack. Phagocytic cells and natural killers are some of the soldiers in the battle of health. The macrophages, a type of white blood cell, literally devour the enemy. Natural killers damage membranes of infected body cells.

In addition to fighting invaders, the body strives to protect itself. Cells that have been "wounded" release a chemical that protects other cells. The body also increases its temperature because the enemy cannot reproduce in extreme heat.

Antibodies come to the rescue when the nonspecific fighting agents don't work. The body produces many varying fighters that are to hook on to an invader and destroy it; the body doesn't initially know what shape will fit. When the right antibody is discovered, the body reproduces it to fight the invader.

The body is designed to remember both the invader and the antibody that worked after it wins the battle. The next time that invader attacks, the body will be better prepared to fight.

It is our duty in this battle to supply the proper amounts of nutrients, rest, and exercise. We can apply the same system to our spiritual body, our soul, and our emotional self. We can arm and protect ourselves against the damaging invaders of discouraging thoughts and feelings.

Before I explain how we can apply the body's immune system to our emotional self, let's talk about our literal emotional response system in the brain. It is very much like our nervous system. Think of what would happen if you tried to pick up a hot knife off the stove. Your brain would immediately signal your fingers to release it. You would have no time to analyze the situation. I explained this in the section about the brain, days 4 and 5. The brain first looks for what will harm it and which mechanisms will keep you safe without the cumbersome process of thinking consciously.

Emotions are meant to act in the same way. I know I've said this before, but it is worth repeating. Your negative emotions are meant to tell you to make changes and motivate you to do something. Unfortunately, sometimes the quick negative emotions that result from difficult circumstances inhibit us from thinking clearly for the best results. Let me repeat that: the quick responses that our bodies need for physical situations are damaging in emotional situations. Quick reactions don't give us access to the thinking skills needed for social situations.

In this section, I will share how you can build a new response mechanism. This new response system will help you act according to your paper brain and upgrade the wiring of your brain more easily. With this new response system, you will first learn to feel with your brain while you rebuild your emotional limbic system.

These are the steps to our bodies' immune system battle plans. We will follow these same steps for our inner selves:

1. Establish self.
2. Recognize invaders.
3. Prevent invaders.
4. Use strategies to fight invaders.
5. Remember the invader and how the battle was won.
6. Take care of ourselves.

Model of "Self"

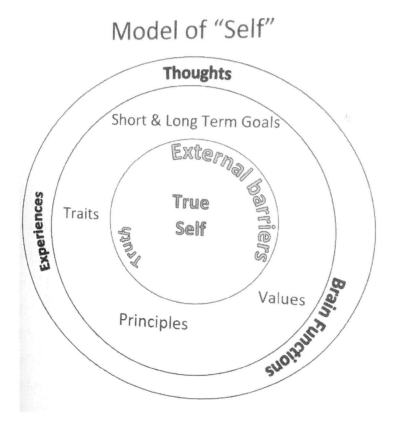

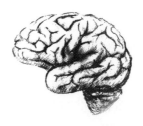

Day 43

Remember to read your brain!!

Establishing Self

To work properly, the physical immune system must know its own cells. It attacks anything that is foreign. For our emotional system to work properly, we need to know our own selves.

When you did the activities to create a paper brain, you established part of your self. True self includes all goals, values, principles, traits, and habits that will bring you lasting happiness—those you have and those you wish to have. The exercise of establishing self (which is true self) will help us act upon the paper brain.

As we consider establishing our true selves, we must keep in mind the desires of our biological brain.

The biological brain wants the following:

- life (oxygen, sleep, food, water)
- reproduction of the species (physical intimacy)
- physical safety and security (shelter, financial security for living, freedom from physical harm)
- emotional stability and safety (belonging)
- positivity (the seeking of rewards, self-fulfillment)

A question you may be thinking is "What does this have to do with establishing who I am?" The answer to this is that your brain doesn't care at all about you and your goals if one of its basic goals for survival is not being met, is threatened, or has the potential to be met. Your brain will emotionally respond to its most basic needs. It is critical to respect this fact as you create who you are.

If you are hungry, eating is your top priority. *Health* isn't. Your brain doesn't care if you want to be a healthy person. If you are single, being with someone is <u>your brain's</u> top priority. *Making a lasting relationship* isn't. Having a companion is paramount. If you are physically threatened, movement toward safety is your top priority. Gracefulness isn't; self-preservation is. If you feel emotionally threatened, doing whatever will help you feel better is your top priority. Tact, accuracy, and others' needs aren't important; self-worth is.

If you are not happy, your brain will not rest until you are happy. You may take a Tylenol, spend time watching YouTube videos, say a sharp word, or eat a piece of chocolate. Your action may relieve the unhappiness caused by the headache, zoning out with YouTube videos may relieve you from a problem at hand, the sharp word may satisfy the anger inside, and the piece of chocolate may satisfy your hunger. These actions don't necessarily solve the problem. You can have only so many Tylenols in a day, avoidance will not protect you forever, you may hurt someone with a sharp word, and too much sugar is rough on your teeth. Your brain will come up with another solution, and then another. The solutions your brain comes up with may not be helpful in the long run. Your brain doesn't care. It isn't omniscient. The brain is not wired with all the knowledge of how to live happily and healthily forever. It is designed, first and foremost, to survive and to reproduce the species. It is designed to get you what you want—easily. The trick, as noted before, is to wire our brains with what we truly want.

Establishing true self for an immune system of the soul will help wire what we truly want to be and prevent downward spirals. The paper brain will help you maintain your true-self goals.

If we were to compare life to climbing mountains, we might say the paper brain gives added security as one climbs. In this analogy, you may have good climbing skills and strong muscles; the paper brain serves as a security rope—something to hang on to as you pull yourself up. The immune system I am going to share with you tomorrow will be a support for when you start to tire or slip. It gives you the desire to keep climbing.

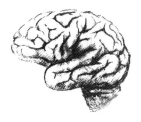

Day 44

Remember to read your paper brain!

Today you will begin to work on the first part of an immune system: establishing self. This exercise will refine the paper brain and is very similar to the making of the brain. As a reminder, the paper brain focuses on action. This section focuses on establishing your true self, which affects the types of actions you want to take in your life.

Allow me to relist the priorities of the real brain:

- life (oxygen, sleep, food, water)
- reproduction of the species (physical intimacy)
- physical safety and security (shelter, financial security for living, freedom from physically harm)
- emotional stability and safety (belonging)
- positivity (the seeking of rewards, self-fulfillment)

The first priority of your brain is physical survival. The second priority of our biological selves is the development of an intimate relationship. Addressing this need of "self" is overwhelmingly essential.

Our minds are strongly wired for attraction. This may seem like a silly thing to think about if you are only eleven or twelve. If you don't establish at a young age the kind of relationship you would like with a spouse, your brain will be attracted to appearances and not give a thought to making the relationship last. All your brain will want is a connection, attention, and someone that looks attractive to you. Consciously decide what you want in a relationship. What are your standards for interacting, communicating, and spending time together? Take some time to think about relationship expectations. I highly recommend that you read some books about developing healthy relationships. What characteristics do you want to develop? If you want to read about preparing yourself for a healthy relationship, write this on your brain wish list.

If you place yourself in intimately romantic places frequently, you will build stronger and stronger desires to have an intimate relationship with whomever you are dating. When your brain has figured out that another person wants to be intimate with you and you want to be intimate with that person, you will have little control in private settings. That is one of the major goals of your brain.

I am not telling you not to have a romantic relationship. I am sharing with you the fact that the more intimate you are—even with kissing—the more your brain takes control of the relationship. It isn't psychology, it is biology. It is not a matter of being spiritually strong enough. If you allow yourself to become physically close to someone that you don't really know, but you think, "This is okay for now," you are putting yourself in a very dangerous situation. Excess time with someone will also alter your thoughts and feelings about the person. Your brain wants a relationship—any kind of relationship. You cannot fight this battle. The only way to keep your goal of finding someone with whom you can have a lasting relationship is to choose now to do things that will promote a healthy relationship. I recommend you carefully consider what is best for you in the long run and then find out how to make sure you do things that will get you what you really want in a relationship.

Maintain an alert mind, and maintain thoughts of your ultimate goal. Write down your standards so you can maintain your goals. Write behaviors or actions you want to do to develop wholesome relationships. Write these on your "true self" list.

For example:

- "I will be intimate only when I'm married."
- "I will be treated respectfully."
- "My significant other will speak kindly to me and enjoy doing things with me."

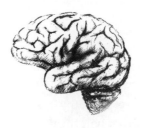

Day 45

Have you read your paper brain today?

Today we are tackling the third priority: belonging and social safety.

For the paper brain, you decided specific things you can do with the people in your life. For the model of your true self, write in the relationships that are most important to you.

The world will provide all kinds of opportunities to interact with other people. It will be easy to develop the fear of missing out. It may be easy to spend a lot of time developing relationships with many people and not developing relationships with those that are most important to you. This is especially true because of the social media platforms at our fingertips. You will need to firmly establish in your mind which relationships are most important to you.

Write the relationships most important to you on your true-self model.

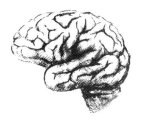

Day 46

How are you doing with your paper brain? Is it getting easier to incorporate your goals? Keep reviewing it!

The Fourth Type of Need of the Brain Is Feeling Capable and Respected

As you consider your true self and the need for feeling capable, there are several things to consider:

- What do you think capability is? What is respectability?
- Who do you want to recognize your capabilities? Whose respect do you want to earn?

Not everyone is going to respect you. People are not perfect, for one. Someone might misunderstand you. In addition, people have varied opinions. Your opinion may or may not be valid. (Remember the story of the Edsel on day 8?) Finally, keep in mind that someone can disagree with you and still respect your opinion.

- Consider all the roles you have in life. For example, child, sibling, employee, student, friend, and member of a group. Write the roles in order from most to least important. What can you do obtain the respect of others in your life?

- To become more capable, what do you do (or wish to do) daily, weekly, and monthly to improve yourself physically, emotionally, intellectually, and spiritually?
- What traits do you wish to develop?

The point is not to be what everyone wants you to be. The point is to find out how you want yourself to be when you are interacting (or will be interacting) with the people in your life. You must be true to your true self; in discovering your true self, it is important that you consider all the roles you have in life.

Compile the list of traits and actions. In the smallest circle of the model of self, write a list of the most repeated significant traits in the space marked "traits." This is one facet of your true self; you may feel you don't have some of these traits, but they are still traits that can develop within you. There may be some traits that you feel you could never develop; don't believe those thoughts. You have decided to build a smart brain. These characteristics represent who you really are or want to be. Your brain is capable of learning to behave the way the real you wants to behave.

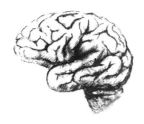

Day 47

This is the fifteenth day you've had your new brain!

The fifth priority of the brain is feeling fulfilled and validated. The brain wants us to feel that we are doing all we are capable of doing. Consider your greatest interests, your wishes according to what you feel is important for happiness, and dreams you have. List them. Put your interests, goals, and desires in order from most to least important.

Write your long-term goals in the area labeled for them. Place them in the outer circle for now. I will explain how you can know when a goal is a goal of your true self. If you currently don't have any long-term goals that you are consciously aware of, leave this area blank.

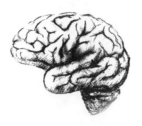

Day 48

Today is day 16 of your paper brain and the final day of establishing your true self.

Today, reflect upon the major choices you have made over the years. Why have you chosen to do what you do, to live as you do, to interact as you do, and to react as you do? Are there any guiding principles of your life that you can identify? If there are any that you know, write them in the section for principles if you wish.

Be continually mindful of the choices you make and how you act, react, and interact. These choices are a result of your principles and beliefs of life. When you know that a certain principle or belief has helped you be your true self and achieve the desires of your true self, put it in your true self area. Reflect upon your self model regularly to internalize it and evaluate your behavior. Use the information from this exercise to help you with your paper brain you made.

The information from these exercises mirrors what you want to become in this life. Perhaps a lot of what you do and hope to do is in line with your real self; on the other hand, there are beliefs and characteristics (for all of us) that are not. These beliefs prevent us from being our true selves. Thus they are to be considered nonself, and as with things that attack our bodies' immune systems, they are to be treated like invaders.

Tomorrow I will explain about emotional invaders.

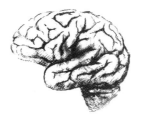

Day 49

Today is day 17 of using your paper brain.

Invaders

Before we talk about invaders, let me review some information. This will help you see why it is important to recognize invaders.

Your biological brain uses priorities to make decisions. Unfortunately, if you are in a stressful situation, the brain decreases certain functions and increases others. As stated earlier, if you are hungry, the brain will only want to focus on getting you food. Physical survival is a priority of the biological brain. For choices that are not physically or socially harmful, do you remember how the brain decides what to do?

The brain does what is *easy* and *rewarding in the given moment*. The paper brain allows you to teach your brain what is most important to you—what your true self feels is most rewarding. When you use it frequently as a guide, you develop stronger neural pathways. This will make it easier for your brain to do what most important instead of what is easy.

Invaders are thoughts, opportunities, and experiences that are easy and appealing but are not helpful in the long run. Preventing invaders from damaging our lives takes two skills: recognizing them and getting rid of them. In the next few days, we will focus on the recognition of invaders.

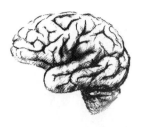

Day 50

Are you still reading your paper brain? Are you using it to make decisions?

Recognizing Invaders

It is by knowing the cells of the self that the body can accomplish the task of recognizing invaders. We can do the same for our minds.

Nonself is any thought, goal, opportunity, or circumstance that does not enhance, help, motivate, or refine the true self. (A circumstance is defined in this book as the social environment one is in.) Nonself cannot be determined strictly by how you feel. I am going to rewrite that statement because it is so important for this section. Nonself cannot be determined strictly by how you feel. Therefore,

Wait! You may already know what I am about to say. Do you remember what we learned about emotions in the first section? I told you we experience emotional reactions based on what is recorded in our brains. Your brain has learned to behave, think, and feel certain ways. It assumes it is right. But as I have explained, it is not always right. I will now go back to my train of thought from before: *Therefore,* we have to think twice about how we feel.

Unfortunately, when we decide to think twice about something and wish to behave or think differently than we might normally, the brain sends a message that the new behavior or belief is wrong. How, for example, could I possibly think well of myself when my brain is wired to believe I am not worth anything? Thinking well of myself would feel wrong if my brain were so wired. Sometimes your opinion or skills may not be very good. And you will do things wrong. Because of this, you will be able to justify your bad feelings about yourself. Think again about this. Does doing something wrong equal being a bad person? If that is the case, we are all bad people!

Your brain may claim you are bad, but this doesn't mean it is true. Just because your brain produces a thought does not make that thought right. I repeat: Just because your brain produces a thought does not make that thought right.

Here is an example: Susie usually takes a nap after dinner. Now she thinks she would rather spend twenty minutes reading. Her body will have adjusted to the routine of a nap at this time. The brain releases a chemical to allow her body to sleep, so it will at first be an uphill climb for her to stay awake.

Changing habits is tough. One of the worst is breaking substance abuse habits, an intensely steep mountain to climb. Anything different from the expectations, habits, goals, and so forth that are recorded in your brain will result in a reaction that will be interpreted as wrong, bad, or impossible in your mind. Likewise, you could feel comfortable about certain behaviors and choices that are contrary to your true self.

Therefore, as stated above, you cannot determine nonself strictly by how you feel. It must be determined by anything that does not enhance, motivate, or refine the true self. You will have to consciously decide what you want to pursue or avoid. In other words, you will need to think about how you are going to feel about something instead of accepting the initial feelings that come from it.

Remember the "think twice" step I shared? (It is on day 24 if you want to review it). When you choose to become smarter than your brain's limbic system, you are willing to think twice and keep ultimate satisfaction in mind as you encounter stimuli (experiences) or have thoughts or wishes to do an action. Invaders will make you feel good about something that really isn't good, or bad about something that will be good for you.

Did you catch that? Invaders make you feel good about bad choices and good about bad choices.

Let me repeat the definition for an invader that I shared earlier: an invader is any thought, goal, opportunity, or circumstance that does not enhance, help, motivate, or refine the true self.

Today I only wanted to give an overview of what an invader is. Tomorrow I will go into more depth. We need to go into more depth because, if your situation is complex, you will need help sorting through what is going on. You will see why reflecting often is important.

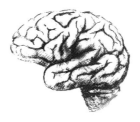

Day 51

Have you done your daily reading of your paper brain?

Today we get to look at specific questions you can ask yourself as you think twice and expose invaders. There are other questions you may develop on your own or learn from others. The main idea is to recognize experiences and thoughts that will only cause you problems in your life.

Remember: an invader is any thought, goal, opportunity, or circumstance that does not enhance, help, motivate, or refine the true self.

Invaders make you want to give up on something wonderful or chase after something wrong. How can you tell what to do? You can start by asking yourself the following questions:

1. Does the thought, goal, opportunity, circumstance, or action *enhance or distract*? In other words, will this keep you on the right track according to your paper brain, or will it only distract you from it? Distractions do not have to be a negative thing; they just take us off course. Distractions are one of the most difficult types of invaders to recognize. They come in the form of wants, usually. We are attracted to things that are appealing, exciting, or personally satisfying. If we do not have true self well established, we can be distracted easily by advertisements, popular schools of thought, and opportunities.

We can be driven in the wind with ever-changing desires or slowly dragged into a lifestyle that is disappointing in the end. Our lives can become filled with insignificant things. The more confident we are in knowing what our true self wants, the easier it will become to identify distracting thoughts, goals, opportunities, actions, and circumstances.

Enhancing opportunities, thoughts, and so forth are those things that we may not have initially planned on but that correlate with our true selves. Perhaps you need to help someone with something. Perhaps an opportunity or job comes up that is even better than the one you had hoped for.

When something entices you, think twice and reflect on your paper brain and model of self. Is it an exciting distraction or truly a good opportunity or goal to pursue? If it is a distraction, keep your eye on your true goals and walk away. If it is a good opportunity, write it somewhere on your paper brain to work toward or do. During your regular reflection time, you can think about how best to begin incorporating your new opportunity.

2. Does it *help or hinder* others or me? This question is an ethical one. Notice I say "hinders." You don't have to help everyone in your path, especially if it hinders you. You may want to sacrifice for someone else. Sacrificing is not necessarily hindering. Sacrificing is simply giving up something for a better reward in the end. Furthermore, true-self actions and thoughts will not hinder others. If you cause someone else to *harmfully* sacrifice for your own benefit, you are developing the trait of selfishness. If you continue to develop this trait, you will begin to willingly do things that harm others. This will create friction in your relationships (with family, at work, and with friends), and others will begin to protect themselves from your destructive behaviors. This may mean strained relations at work—or maybe even getting fired or losing friendships. The true self does not develop itself at the expense of others.

I must again point out that this does not mean you have to do everything for everyone else; this question gives you time to see whether it hinders you, too. Abuse, for example, may be hindering you but may allow another to do as they wish. Others may make you think that you are helping them by enduring weaknesses they have. This is not so. You are not helping them change. In such cases, you are communicating to them that the behavior is okay when it is not.

Recognize behaviors that hinder you as invaders. We'll learn in a few days how to apply a plan of attack to react appropriately to invaders.

3. Does it *refine or burn?* This question is similar to the second one. The second focuses on thoughts and actions that may affect others. This one is good to ask regarding circumstances, ideas, goals, opportunities, and actions that may be difficult for us. Our brains react negatively to the things it cannot do easily or that lack an emotional attachment. Because of this, there are some negative feelings we must endure until we begin to feel positive emotions from achieving what we desire.

On the other hand, we do not have to sacrifice or endure all things (such as abuse, as mentioned above). If there are thoughts, goals, circumstances, or actions that you know have no benefit to you in the end, they are nonself. For this reason, we sometimes need to

   a) say no to some opportunities, ideas, invitations, and the like;
   b) get out of or stay away from some circumstances; and
   c) ignore some thoughts.

Keep in mind that we are learning and that we don't always recognize the things that will burn us. Alternatively, we may think that something will burn us and want to steer clear of it, when in reality it is a genuine opportunity for growth with huge personal rewards. If something is going to tear you down physically, emotionally, or mentally, consider it an invader.

4. Does it *motivate or deflate*? This question helps distinguish thoughts and circumstances as true self or nonself. Do you have thoughts that are justifiable in your mind but keep you from doing what you would like to do? Are there people around you that say or do things that hurt and discourage you? Are you in circumstances that are discouraging? It is important to know that that the circumstances, actions, and sayings of others can be enemies. People are not our enemies. We are learning to attack invaders, not people. Sometimes we must withdraw ourselves from people because we cannot control what they say or do. We can control only ourselves.

If you are experiencing discouraging circumstances, the next section will help you prevent deflation. Be true to yourself. Expect and accept only things that motivate and help you, even your own thoughts. Did you see that? *Even your own thoughts!* I know your mind can produce some pretty convincing thoughts. In a few days, I will explain how to think the right thoughts and get rid of those false, persuasive thoughts.

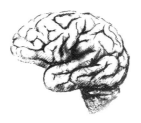

Day 52

Are you still using your paper brain to make decisions?

Can you remember the questions I suggested you start thinking about? They are as follows:

1. Does this enhance or distract? Invaders distract. Oh yeah, they look like good things to pursue, but they aren't on your paper brain or self model. So write these thoughts or ideas down if need be, but don't put time, money, or thought into them unless you realize they really are part of your true self.
2. Does this help or hinder? Invaders hinder people. No one needs to improve his or her life by ruining yours. Likewise, be careful not to do things that make you feel better at the expense of others.
3. Does this refine or burn? Demands that provide growth are welcome. Anything else is an invader.
4. Does this motivate or deflate? All deflating thoughts, media, and words of others are invaders, period.

The above questions help you look objectively at negative feelings and overcome them. The first question helps you see which positive feelings or opportunities can inhibit you because they can be a distraction. The third one helps you realize that negative feelings sometimes accompany good opportunities because they stretch us, and stretching doesn't always feel good!

Notice that none of the filtering questions are "Is it realistic or not?" The brain does not have the full ability to see what we are capable of or what opportunities are going to come into our lives.

Q: But what if I *do* have a truly unrealistic goal? What if it really is stupid or too hard? What if I'm pursuing something truly impossible for *me*? I don't want to waste time on an impossible goal.

A: No, you don't want to waste time on a goal that is so difficult for you to obtain that you never seem to make progress. So if there is something you wish you could have but it just doesn't seem realistic, this is what I recommend:

1. Go ahead and keep the goal. After all, it is truly what you want. It is true to you. If you eliminate it from your true-self model, you are not giving your brain the opportunity to figure out a way to make it happen. It will never seem realistic or give you the opportunity to achieve the goal that you could've achieved as you pursued the "unrealistic" goal.
2. Set short-term goals based on what you are in control of and what will help you work toward the impossible goal. For example, let's say you want to buy an expensive home someday. Address this in a helpful, realistic way. What can you do to save money now? What can you do to earn money now or in the future?

Remember: don't ignore desires because they seem unrealistic. Ignore them because they are destructive and nonself.

Q: What if I set a goal that I think is realistic (or I am willing to believe it is) and nothing is happening? How long do I wait before I can genuinely give up?

A: The steps toward a true goal will always be made on true-self pathways. In other words, you will be doing things that enhance, motivate, help, or refine. If you cannot pursue a goal without feeling as though it is a distraction from more important goals, or if you are deflated, burned or hindered, then you are pursuing a goal that is not good. You don't give up on goals; you abandon wrong ones! If nothing is happening but the pursuit of the goal is enhancing and refining your life, never, ever give up. You may decide to change the amount of time you spend on it, but the first rule of living your life awake is to not stop pursuing a true goal just because you aren't getting results you want when you want them. The deflating thought is "It is taking too long." Our brains don't know how long it will take.

Note: The pursuit of a goal should not drain you financially or emotionally. Otherwise, it is burning you. Evaluate your actions: are you doing the wrong actions to pursue the right goal? After all, we are all learning. Life is trial and error.

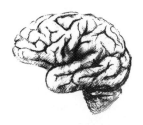

Day 53

Are you tired of me asking you about your paper brain?

To further aid you in the recognition stage, below are some insights to help in diagnosing negative feelings that come when you are trying to do what is best in the long run.

These are negative (uncomfortable) feelings that we experience as we try to be our true selves:

1. Allergic reaction: This type of feeling is a result of trying to be our true selves. You may experience a time when your personality or way of thinking has a negative outcome. This happens because principles and behaviors sometimes don't apply well. Let me give you an example: A person may have great leadership skills and know how to take charge when something needs to get done. However, always taking charge can be counterproductive. Sometimes a person needs to stand back and let another learn skills of decision-making, delegating, and advising. When we apply principles of direct leadership at a time when guidance is needed, problems and negative feelings may arise. In this example, being bold and giving direction isn't bad. Many leaders throughout history have stood up and boldly proclaimed their stances on things that have brought about needed changes, and they have led groups through crises. However, being strong-willed and bold

is less effective when a loved one needs an understanding, listening ear or an employee has an idea you need to learn more about. As a youth, being strong-willed can help you maintain your beliefs for healthy habits (in such ways as saying no to drugs, alcohol, and cigarettes, and resisting temptations that lead to unhealthy relationships), and you will be able to live a life free of addictions. However, being strong-willed is dangerous at times when you don't see what others around you *do* see. You may ignore counsel that you think is childish or irrelevant because you want to be "treated as an adult." In the end, you may find that your strong belief in your ability to choose a good path was harmful in the end, and that had you been willing to be open-minded, you could have saved yourself some degree of heartache.

Again, being confident in your abilities isn't bad. Being bold isn't bad. Being submissive isn't bad. Being quiet isn't bad. Being extremely social isn't bad. Being funny isn't bad. Being serious isn't bad. There are many types of personalities and traits; learn to appreciate your strengths. When bad feelings come about because of your personality or beliefs, reflect on how you can build other traits as well. Learn when your strengths are needed most. Don't assume that you are bad or that others are bad or wrong. Eventually, this attitude, which is an invader because it deflates, will also cause you problems.

Review the section about personalities (day 9) to appreciate who you are while respecting others as well.

2. Withdrawal symptoms: These are feelings that come about as a direct result of trying to change and eliminate poor behaviors. Your mind will think that it is wrong to stop any habit, even if the habit is bad. Others around you may also act negatively because you are not doing the things they expect of you. Be firm.

3. Feeling sore: When you introduce a new physical activity, you may experience sore muscles. Likewise, as you increase

the positive things you do, your mind will have a negative reaction because you are requiring it to do something it is not accustomed to doing. Be strong. Be smarter than your brain. Keep going!

The above are guidelines to help you. Life is complex, and solutions will sometimes not be easy to discover. Please maintain your commitment for ultimate satisfaction. Solutions will come, even if they come slowly at first. How do I know? Because the brain is designed to help you obtain what it wants. When you stay committed to your goals, your brain will eventually adopt them and think of ways to achieve them.

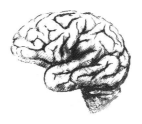

Day 54

I've challenged you to daily review your brain model. Now you have another model to reflect upon: your true self. Reflect upon this model once a week for as long as it takes to make it a part of your memory and life. Once you feel it is a natural part of your thinking, keep it fresh in your mind by looking at it monthly.

If you have not been reviewing your brain model each day, why is this? Have you found your own system? Have you not had time for it? If time is an issue, put the brain model in a convenient place or take a snapshot of it. Any time you have a moment (such as while stopped at a traffic light or sitting in a waiting room), look at it. Think about it. Memorize it and think about it throughout the day. Think about it when you are going to and from places or when getting ready for the day. These are just ideas for making it a part of you. Whatever you do, the point is to keep your working memory aware of what *you* say is important, not what your brain has recorded as important.

Remember: the more effective your working memory and the truer the expectations, goals, principles, habits, and traits you have biologically recorded, the greater your chances of being successful in your endeavors.

Today, take the time now to look at the model of your self.

- Consider your goals and typical behaviors.

- Ask the four "think twice" questions from day 52.
- Place all the things that you know to be your true self in the inner circle.

Think about your behavior. Are you getting closer to your true self? Are you staying true to your goals? Are you developing and following the types of principles that are healthy? As a way of noting progress, put a star or check by those traits that have become biologically recorded. Write down principles that you have learned since you began using your paper brain.

Now that you have learned how to identify what is nonself, it is necessary to know how to *prevent* nonself stimuli from stopping your progress and affecting how you feel. I mentioned earlier that sometimes our own thoughts can try to stop our progress, and I promised I would address this. That topic begins tomorrow!

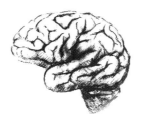

Day 55

Review your paper brain!

Prevention: External Barriers

Our bodies have ways to prevent us from getting sick. In other words, you are healthy because your body has protected you from many viruses and bacteria that could have made you sick. We are constantly in contact with things that can make us feel ill.

We are also constantly bothered with things that can discourage us. Like the body's immune system, we can develop a personality that reacts and acts well even under difficult circumstances. There are many healthy traits that are good; seven crucial ones are laid out below.

These external barriers come from studying the counsel of religious leaders. I reviewed dozens of articles about happiness, noting the counsel given. Eventually I began to see a pattern. The traits I have listed are the traits the leaders recommended. I pondered their words and created these descriptions.

Why Are the External Barriers So Important?

We react and act according to what is in our brains. Therefore, to have the most correct responses, we must have the information stored along a well-insulated neurological pathway that can process the stimuli correctly. These external barriers offer you some correct information.

Reading about these is only the beginning. You will have to permanently record this information in your mind by reviewing it frequently and applying it. You may already understand many or most of these truths.

Years ago, I kept a list of these traits handy; if I felt poorly, I would refer to the list to see whether there was a trait I could apply to keep from getting stuck in an emotional rut. I found I had to work on having a sense of humor and staying determined. Read about these traits over the coming days, and consider which traits you would like to improve.

Trait 1: A Sense of Humor

A sense of humor eases troubles that arise.[12]

- Fact 1: Bad things happen often.
- Fact 2: When we focus on something, we allow it to create a pathway in our brain.
- Conclusion: If we get upset about bad things that happen, we will reinforce the connections and mechanisms that produce our negative emotions. If we instead have a sense of humor, we can reinforce positive feelings.

If something bad happens or someone does or says something negative, quickly think twice and decide if it is something temporary. If it is temporary, look at the lighter side of things. Anger, with or without a cause, cannot survive long in these conditions. When a moment of disappointment crosses your path, step right over it with some humor. Don't build on it and create an insurmountable thought pattern. What if you have a bad hair day, your teacher is a bit impatient, a sibling bothers you, or someone forgets to do something for you? The list could go on. All these events are temporary, so keep them temporary. Don't let them create permanent damage by staying angry.

Sometimes you can't really find humor in the situation, but you can at least see its temporary nature. Treat the problem as if it's a mosquito bite; leave it alone, and eventually the body will heal from it. Otherwise, the scratching of it will make it spread. Learn to let it go.

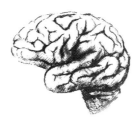

Day 56

You have had a paper brain for about twenty days now. How are you doing? Don't give up on it; actually, don't give up on *you*.

Today's message is about external barrier 2.

Trait 2: Be Willing to Step into the Unknown because You Know It Is a Good Thing to Do[13]

Acting on inspirations or deductive reasoning is often referred to as faith. Faith is a manifestation of the willingness to do something that you feel a little confident of although you are uncertain of the outcome. You are stepping (moving forward in action) into the unknown (the results of your action) because you know it is what you should do (owing to reasoning, former teaching, or a divine impression). This attitude prevents feelings of hopelessness and stops us from doing things that will thwart our progress; it gives us the strength to do the things that will lead us to desired opportunities.

Think about what I've taught you about the brain. We know that the brain is not aware of everything. We know our brains pick up many signals and analyzes them. The brain checks to determine whether something is going to harm us. It checks to determine whether there is a reward or punishment for a particular action. It learns what it is capable of and which things pose threats.

Let's think about those facts in relation to the moment when you desire to do something that your brain

- has never seen you do before,
- cannot deduce that you can learn to do, or
- has erroneously learned will go against what it already assumes is right.

Do you think your brain is going to send a happy *"Go for it!"* thought and emotion in that moment? No, it will not. It will tell you, "Stop. Do not try this. Quit. Forget it." But is the brain always right? No. So it is necessary, at times, to communicate to our brains that we can learn to do what we want to do or that an idea isn't as bad as it may sound. We may have to take the time to think about the facts we know to prove it will be okay if we proceed with our plans.

This very idea is illustrated in research conducted by Joseph LeDoux from Cornell University in New York. Studying the fear response in search of a way to help victims recover from traumatic experiences, LeDoux has taught rats to retrain the amygdala's response to a stimulus that would typically yield a freeze response. The rats are slowly conditioned to keep moving to eliminate a tone that the rats have been previously conditioned to fear.

As humans, we can do the same. We can step forward and reroute our thinking and abilities. Keep your ultimate goals in focus. Keep your values and principles in focus. For example, if you have ever found it hard to tell the truth, that is because your mind doesn't see how telling the truth can possibly be helpful—even though you may have been taught that lying is wrong. It takes a "willingness to step into the unknown" to tell the truth. Your friends that succumb to peer pressure are either more concerned about being accepted now (immediate satisfaction) than about any future results, or they do not see any future reward for withstanding the temptation.

Biologically speaking, we rob ourselves of the opportunity to show our brains the rewards of acting on what we know when we are not willing to step into the unknown.

Endurance (sometimes called "grit") is needed when we begin to tire in our efforts to be smarter than our brain; faith, on the other hand, is needed when we hold back efforts because we don't have all the answers. There will be times when your faith (or willingness to take a risk based on what you know) will be tried. You must understand that there are so many factors and complexities in life that sometimes we innocently misinterpret people and misjudge circumstances and possibilities. Interestingly, we understand the concept of faith when we watch movies and read novels. We are thrilled with unpredictable climaxes and rejoice when the heroes or heroines succeed amid obstacles.

As you live out your own success story, you will encounter many intense moments. These can become climaxes to a great chapter of your life. Your willingness to act on what you know is essential to creating a happy and successful ending.

This means that once you have established the goals and principles of your true self, you should never doubt them again. Act on them. I repeat: unless you know without a doubt that something you have identified as true self is not right, *do not doubt your true self, true character, or true goals.* Do not allow uncertainty about a result or a process rob you of success. No matter what your goals in life, there will always be something out there to challenge them. You will always have struggles in developing good habits or achieving any good goal. You might as well stick to your true self. Keep the faith.

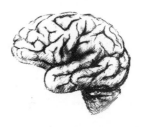

Day 57

Are you trying to use more humor and faith in your life?

This next trait will take some faith, and a sense of humor will help you out.

Trait 3: Be Satisfied in Waiting for Results of Your Actions or for More Information before Acting or Reacting[14]

Be patient. This does not mean that we must sit around in misery, hoping to eventually get what we want. That isn't patience. That is waiting. Waiting is freezing your life. Waiting yields bitterness. Waiting doesn't make dreams come sooner; it blinds you to possibilities. Patience brings about peace of mind. Patience understands that things take time; it opens your eyes to opportunities.

We all take time to learn and grow. Be patient with yourself. Be patient with those around you. Be patient with life. Take a deep breath and do not act or react on limited information.

- What if a friend of mine tells me something negative about someone else? What is my reaction? A natural first reaction is to have a negative emotion or thought. So what will I *choose* as my next reaction—what will I choose to think and feel?
- What about the times when others say something that is negative about me? How will I react?

- What if someone disagrees with me? When this happens, will I keep talking—without any negative feelings—for complete understanding of their opinion? Will I listen to the person's needs? Will I express myself in a non-attacking way?
- What if I do something that causes a problem? How will I react? Will I be patient with myself?

When we are patient, we prevent problems from escalating and situations from spiraling downward. We keep doors open for positive things to still take place. For example, if I am not patient with the amount of time it takes to complete a task, I will abandon the task. As a result, I will never realize the goal of achieving that task.

Patience is being satisfied with delayed results related to something we are working on, including ourselves! It is being satisfied with the progress of others. It is postponing initial negative feelings about something or someone until we get more information. It is seeking to understand. It requires open-mindedness. As a result of being patient, we will reinforce positive networks instead of negative ones.

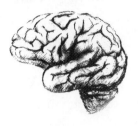

Day 58

Today's trait is one of the most frequently discussed in today's inspirational messages in speeches and books.

Trait 4: Show That You Feel an Inner Joy for the Things You Have Been Given and Things You Can Do

Be grateful.[15] This attitude is of great help when it seems nothing in life is going to get any better, when all seems hopeless. Notice that this trait is more than a feeling; it is an expression of a feeling. It is applied by not habitually complaining; it is manifested by deeds of kindness and demonstrated in our tones of voice and interactions with others. Gratitude is apparent when one uses talents to lift others and rejoices in the talents of others.

There is another important reason to be genuinely grateful for what you have. Without it, you will never, ever be happy—never—because your mind isn't designed to naturally be happy about what you have. Nope. Go back and read what your brain does. It looks for what will harm it and what will help it get a reward. Your mind is constantly on the lookout for these two things. When you get a reward, your mind will cause a surge of great feelings. These will fade, and your mind will be back to seeking a reward or protecting you from harm. You must consciously decide to feel a continual peace or happiness for what you've accomplished so far in life.

As people pursue their lives, they may receive or accomplish many things. As stated earlier, no one is ever handed freely *exactly* what he or she needs to succeed. The grateful person uses what she has while working toward what she wants or needs, and then she genuinely appreciates every step toward progress.

Look around at your life. Life may be very dark. Exercise gratitude by imagining there is a light at the end of your dark tunnel and each day you are getting closer to it. With this trait, you will not be walking in the dark for long.

Day 59

Today I share two traits: humility and forgiveness. The first helps us apply the second.

Trait 5: You Don't Know Everything, and Everyone You Meet Knows Something You Don't[16]

This trait, known as "being teachable" or "humility," is one of the simplest to develop and keep. Nonetheless, this trait will save you a lot of mistakes and will hurry you along your path of success. Learn, learn, learn. Learn about your goals. Learn about the things on your paper brain. The more you know, and the more you dwell on what you know, the more capable your brain is to naturally act as you wish. The more information you have for your working memory to consider, the wiser your choices will be.

In addition to the above benefits, you will develop a personality that is pleasant to be around. After all, it is very dissatisfying to be around someone that does not respect you and what you know. Remember: the brain assumes it is right about everything. To balance this out, consciously think twice and notice what others think, feel, and know. By doing so, you will learn better principles of living and better ideas to achieve your dreams and avoid pitfalls.

Trait 6: Forgive Yourself and Others; Forget the Pain but Remember the Lesson[17]

This can be a tough trait to keep when you have been wronged. Someone may have created the darkness you are in. How do we approach problems like this?

Keep this in mind: you do not have mental energy to waste on someone or something that has already hurt you. You have things to do and places to go. If you dwell on the pain, you will build a strong neurological pathway, and that is where your thoughts will often go. If you do not forget the pain, you may trigger the thought each time it is associated with a future hurt. Forgive and forget the pain, but do not forget the lesson. You do not want to be hurt again. If circumstances are such that you are continually disrespected (through abuse of some kind), then write one of your short- or long-term goals to change that environment.

For less damaging circumstances, it is good to remember no one is perfect. Besides, we all think differently! Try to understand the other's perspective, or simply know in your heart that he or she may or may not mean to be hurtful. Seek understanding instead of revenge.

Remember the questions I proposed: "What is my perspective?" and "What is truth?" In finding truth, try looking at the perspective of the other person or persons. I'm not suggesting that you are always wrong. I know that our brains do not see everything. Perhaps if we could look at or listen to others' perspectives, we might not feel as offended, angry, or hurt.

Keep in mind that forgiveness also applies to the daily mistakes you make. No one is perfect. Forgive yourself. Remember the lesson.

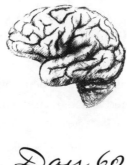

Day 60

This is the final trait that I constantly worked on.

Trait 7: Keep Going![18]

The trait of persistence is the vehicle for your success story. It has a gas pedal but no reverse gear. The more you apply the gas pedal, the faster you'll get to where you wish to go. This trait is a nice balance to patience. Patience makes long rides pleasant. Persistence prevents the trip from being any longer than it needs to be!

At those times when you are a little bored with your story's plot or you are beginning to tire from doing what you know you must do, be persistent. Keep on; don't stop. Your brain may tell you to quit via thoughts and feelings. If you are doing something that is important according to your true self, don't change anything. Keep going. If your brain had a certain task biologically recorded as being vital, it wouldn't matter how boring or tiring the task became. Your brain would push you to keep on. The brain analyzes the situation, realizes it must push forward, and then signals the body to exert the energy to do so.

When you have identified something as important, do it. Don't give up before it is recorded well. When this finally happens, the task will be easier to do. In the meantime, be persistent.

You have now learned the external barriers for your soul's immune system. These are traits that prevent unnecessary feelings and actions that stop or thwart your progress.

1. Have a sense of humor.
2. Have faith.
3. Be patient with yourself and others.
4. Be grateful.
5. Be teachable.
6. Be forgiving of yourself and others.
7. Be determined.

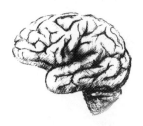

Day 61

On days 55–60 I shared the traits I incorporate in my life to prevent me from feeling down. I am not suggesting you don't have these qualities. I'm also not suggesting that these are the only traits we need to develop. These are simply traits I discovered from research, and they made a significant difference in my life. I encourage you to consider what traits (external barriers) you have that help you. What others do you feel are important to develop?

I made a list of these traits and read them daily. I used them in times of emotional challenges. When feeling a negative emotion, I would think quickly about the traits, looking for one that I could apply.

In addition to determination and humor, an external barrier I needed to develop was patience with myself. I used to get frustrated and want to give up too easily.

I used humor to deal with mistakes I made. For example, when I made mistakes in the past, the words "I'm so stupid" came naturally into my mind. To deal with this, I started thinking, "I'm so stupid … but I'm not dumb!" I know "dumb" and "stupid" mean the same thing, but "I'm so stupid" was such a quick response, and I had to make a joke of it somehow and change my thinking. Today, I don't deal with the "I'm stupid" reaction.

Sometimes I feel I am just not good enough at something. I remember I simply need time to learn more (to be teachable). This puts my weaknesses or inabilities in perspective, causing negative feelings to subside.

To prevent a negative feeling from spreading too deep or far into my life, I envision the negative feeling as a wound and think of an appropriate bandage. If the emotional pain is the result of an action I took, I will "fix" the problem as best I can and apply the bandage of forgiving myself. Likewise, if someone else did something that hurt me, I apply the bandage of forgiveness and address the issue appropriately. Think of a time when you got cut. It really hurt at first, didn't it? Eventually the pain subsided. Because of habituation, emotions can subside as well.

Yes, like pain, all feelings are indicators and motivators; pay attention to them, but don't let them rule you. Place the "external barrier" traits list somewhere you can read it often. Still, even when we are conscious about developing positive traits, sometimes debilitating feelings or the negative actions of others persist. When this is the case, get ready for attack!

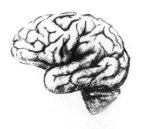

Day 62

I've tried to help you create your paper brain and model of self to review daily. The model of self reflects what you think. The paper brain reflects what you want to do. Use these to guide your feelings. In the last few days, we've talked about how you can have peace in your life. However, let's face it; life is messy, and we are, as the singer Mandisa puts it, "Unfinished." We have thoughts and behaviors that are hardwired in our minds, and it will take some time to weed out what we don't want to think or do anymore.

For the next few days, we'll talk about how to attack the negative emotions that come regularly or don't seem to go away. For today, take some time to review the external barriers so you can understand them better and think about how you can apply them.

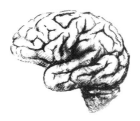

Day 63

In the recognition stage, we take the time to ask questions to identify opportunities, experiences, and thoughts that are harmful or are nonself. Remember: nonself thoughts and experiences deflate, burn, hinder, and distract us. Wouldn't it be great if we could immediately recognize all harmful behaviors and thoughts? It would be just as wonderful if we already had developed all the external barriers to stop those harmful behaviors or thoughts!

Plan of Attack

We are still growing, so we will encounter nonself thoughts and experiences that threaten our peace of mind and our life journeys. Life isn't simple, and we don't know all truths. It is very difficult in the first place to even recognize nonself, so by the time we are beginning to realize the problems in our lives because of nonself actions and thoughts, it often feels as if it is too late to do anything. But it is not. This isn't the time to give up. This is the time to *attack*. Our physical immune systems don't give up when invaders begin to hurt our bodies. They continue to fight. We can do the same for our souls.

In the *physical body*, the immune system has two stages for the fighting of an invader:

1. Destruction of foreign substances by nonspecific fighters (the white blood cells)
2. Inactivating foreign substances by specific fighters (the antibodies)

For our *emotional or mental selves*, these are the two stages of fighting invaders:

1. Incorporating positive stimuli in your life (thoughts and actions that help our minds focus better)
2. The implementation of specific ideas we learn from others

I will first explain stage 1 on day 63. Stage 1 helps with less-serious issues and boost your spirits. The aid of positive stimuli addresses the need for maintaining a positive feeling.

The goal of the immune system of the soul is to improve our lives by eliminating negative feelings that cripple us. Some negative feelings are a result of circumstances that need to be changed and not a result of our actions or thoughts. I understand this. Not everything going on in your life is a result of something you've done. However, you will need to eliminate negativity to free your mind and figure out what to do to get out of your circumstances. This step of the immune system (the attack) allows our brains' full power to be used to process and retrieve information. We've got to fight the negative thoughts and feelings that occur, so we can have the strength and thoughts to make the necessary changes in our lives.

Some persons have internal situations that make it difficult to be happy; these are persons with brains that function atypically. Every one of us has beliefs or thoughts that are not healthy. A person with an atypical brain has a more difficult time processing incoming stimuli. Nevertheless, whether you have the task in life of overcoming an atypical brain or not, learning how to attack nonself items will help alleviate some of your negative feelings.

Let me first explain the science behind this phase. I want to convince your mind, right now, that the steps of this stage are worth the effort. The prefrontal cortex, which is the area that analyzes data in your brain and regulates emotions, is divided into two sections: positive and negative. Research shows that a person with depression has a dominating right cortex, and Richard Davidson (a neuroscientist at the University of Wisconsin's Health Emotions Research Institute) recommends, among other interventions, that these persons set the simplest goals (such as leaving their home at a certain time) and reflecting upon their achievements.[19] These very simple activities stimulate the positive circuits in the brain.

The overall goal of the attack phase is to allow the left side of the brain to have circuits that are as strong as possible. You may recall that strengthening a neuronal path requires us only to repeat an action or thought often. This appears to be too good to be true, but it is a scientific fact.

For our emotional immune system, I compare positive experiences with the white blood cells. Just as the physical body fights invaders with white blood cells, our mental selves—controlled by the brain—need experiences that naturally boost the brain's ability to feel positive.

White blood cells are helpful, but they are victorious only if there are more of them than the invader. They multiply rapidly and get to work before the enemy spreads.

Equally, we must increase the number of positive stimuli to exceed the negative ones we are experiencing or feeling. Therefore, the focus is on *what to do*, not on what to stop feeling. And the goal is to outnumber the negative stimuli with positive stimuli.

Because the brain responds to us, we can train it to think and act. And guess what—we don't even have to have a positive attitude to do it! Amazing, isn't it? We need only focus on doing positive things and think positive thoughts, and the brain will start making us feel positive. I can do the simplest acts, and the brain will respond favorably. Seriously.

The trouble is, it does take effort; when you are feeling down, effort is very unappealing. To be sure, doing positive things when you are feeling down feels impossible, doesn't it? This is why these things are so appealing and addictive:

- caffeine
- shopping
- overeating
- alcohol and nicotine
- unhealthy relationships
- playing electronic games
- anger

These give immediate gratification—immediate relief from the pain. Reaching into a bag of food or opening a can of pop takes so little effort to offer immediate results in comparison with the ideas you will read in the following sections. So if the above things are so effective and easy, why not put them on the list of ideas for attacking nonself? (You will find the list on day 64.)

In the immune system for the soul and for the body, the white blood cells are meant to protect the self. All the ideas listed above, though they give immediate relief, will eventually cause more troubles. They do not bring feelings of peace for the brain to think better.

Advertisers and even friends may try to convince you that these things are harmless. Your own brain may even make you think they are okay. But you can be smarter than your brain. You do not have to listen to your brain; make your brain listen to you!

Attacking is the act of doing or thinking something that stimulates a positive feeling in the brain. The following sections offer ideas for attacking nonself thoughts and feelings in ways that are not damaging to your true self.

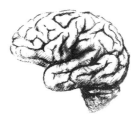

Day 64

Yesterday I introduced the phase of attack, which relates to actions you do when you are burdened with negative thoughts and feelings. The attack phase of the body's immune system has two parts: (1) Our bodies have white blood cells to fight foreign materials that come into them; these are general, nonspecific fighters. (2) Our bodies also fight by using specific blood proteins known as antibodies. I will now spend a few days talking about our souls' white blood cells.

The soul's white blood cells are positive experiences and thoughts. I will share some of these today. There are many ideas for families, relationships, and general living. You can find lots of ideas for positive experiences in magazines and books, on the internet, and in classes.

The key ideas about white-blood-cell experiences are as follows:

1. Simple positive experiences need to frequently fill your life. Your brain needs them to function toward successful behavior. If you don't offer positive, enriching opportunities for your brain, it will most likely get stuck because of the stresses that come into your life. You will be influenced by negativity in your culture. Your brain's ability to function successfully is in your hands. Remember: you can't fight negativity with more negativity. Fill your life with simple positive experiences.

2. Positive experiences need to be intentional. You will need to be willing to do positive things without feeling positive

sometimes. Yes, negative feelings are often valid, but learn to concentrate on your actions. A long time ago, I had to do this regularly. There was no way I could talk myself into feeling better. I smiled, cleaned, and even focused on breathing sometimes. Sometimes I would think about happy memories. I focused on doing or thinking something different and did not waste time trying to tell myself it is wrong to feel bad. Because I did this, today negative feelings no longer paralyze me; this technique has been very helpful. Instead of dwelling on negative events, my focus is always on my present behavior.

3. Positive experiences should be planned even in times when things are going well. These will reinforce the positive neurological pathways and, most importantly, create and maintain healthy relationships. Fill your life with positive traditions and routines. Many of the things you listed on the paper brain are examples of white blood cells because they are things you want to accomplish. There are many spontaneous things you can do as well; for example, you can leave notes for your parents, take five minutes to clean up a part of the house, or take time out to talk with a sibling.

Below are two lists of "white blood cell" experiences: routine ones and emergency ones. These are simply suggestions to give you ideas; you will want to find what works for you. Routine experiences are those you do regularly to keep your immune system strong. Some of the actions you have on your paper brain act as white blood cells. The activities of the emergency list can be applied in moments of disappointment, sadness, or anger.

Routine White Blood Cell Experiences—Actions to Incorporate on a Regular Basis[20]

1. Exercise. I'm not talking about major workouts at the gym. There are a lot of simple ideas of things you can do at home;

in fact, you can even do in-chair exercises! Movement offers a great emotional boost.

2. Read positive literature. Pick something out from the library if you don't have any money to buy a book. Have this material in accessible areas. Like exercising, this white blood cell is best when regularly applied. For example, some people regularly read religious material. In great challenging times, you can increase your dosage of this white blood cell.

3. Plan and do acts of kindness. Research studies suggest that developing compassion is beneficial to one's well-being.

4. Write. Start a journal to express yourself. Don't know what to say? Write the things you wish you could talk to someone about. You don't have to make sense. But be cautious; it is okay to vent, but at the same time, you don't want to strengthen negative thoughts too much. In the past, I would write "Right now I'm feeling [this emotion] because [of this reason]. I know this will not last forever."

5. Create something. Color! Do an art or craft project. Bake. Take out paper and pencil and design your future home or write about your future career.

6. Socialize *in person*! Play games with someone.

Emergency White Blood Cell Experiences—
Actions to Incorporate in Challenging Moments

Because you won't feel like doing anything positive when you are upset, emergency WBC experiences are quick things to do to keep positive neuron connections active in challenging moments. I recommend you plan what you want to do so you can be prepared.

1. Picture nature or something you love.

2. Make a list of things, such as things you're thankful for (be creative and be humorous), things you like doing, things you will do someday, or things that are important to you. Make a mental list if you don't have paper.

3. Think of what you would like to do for a day with a certain person in your life.
4. Think about a dream-come-true experience you would like to have.
5. Smile. You don't have to feel like smiling. You can hate smiling. Simply doing it will stimulate all the things that are associated with smiling.
6. Munch on something healthy. (Put veggies or fruits on your grocery list!)
7. Listen to instrumental music or music with positive lyrics. Sing along. Dance along!
8. Use mindfulness techniques, such as deep breathing.

These are just a few ideas of positive things you can do to counteract the negative. The purpose of doing these simple actions is to allow your mind to better focus on improvement. If you stay focused on the negative, your mind won't be able to concentrate on a solution or help the negative feelings go away.

I know this all sounds so easy and reasonable—until you are in the moment. There were times when I didn't even *want* to feel positive again. And such times even occurred while I was working on this book! When this happened, I would challenge myself to do the necessary tasks of life without changing my present ugly attitude or feelings. I would count the number of things I could do (or how much time could pass) while still feeling rotten about life. In the challenge, I didn't try to change how I felt. I challenged myself to be motivated by what I "felt" in my mind instead of my heart. If you would like to try this challenge, when feeling negative, start the timer. See how long you can stay angry or sad. It always helped me, and I was always so grateful I didn't give in to the negative feelings and thoughts in my heart.

Tomorrow I will share the second part of the attack phase.

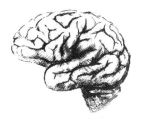

Day 65

Your body produces antibodies to attack specific invaders. For the soul, antibodies are specific truths we can apply to a problem. We can learn from our mistakes and those of others. Many books have been written to address specific problems and offer solutions. One book cannot even begin to share all the truths you will need to know.

Thankfully, many people have been inspired to share truths; their words seem to touch our hearts in just the right way.

After talking today about general deflating thoughts, in the next few days I want to share my thoughts about four specific invaders: "This is too difficult for me," "It is impossible for me to change," "I can't resist," and "This isn't working."

Attacking Deflating Invaders

Today you will learn things you can do when you are feeling blue! (Reading your paper brain and model of self is one of them. Did you read or think about yours today?)

Usually, the last thing you want to do when things are not going well or you feel down is to think positive thoughts. You need changes. You need help. You need support. You need lifting. Thinking positive when you are in difficult circumstances feels like being asked to fix a skinned-up knee while your hands are bleeding profusely. It feels impossible, as if it is a waste of time and an avoidance of the real issue.

So why would I suggest thinking positive when it feels impossible and worthless? Because it only *feels* worthless. It is not worthless.

Sometimes when I found it hard to think positive, I would write about the negative thoughts to acknowledge them. I would then think, "Yes, these may be true, but negative thoughts have never helped me." I would ignore those negative truths and move on. It was easier to just *not think* the negative things than it was to try to think positively. I could think the phrase "Yes, these may be true, but negative thoughts have never helped me" because I had learned it was undeniably true. Dwelling on the negative thoughts never did help me improve.

That was my go-to antibody that put me on the path to recovering from the negative feelings and thoughts: *negative thoughts have never helped me.*

When it seems impossible to ignore the negative or pull a positive thought into your mind, consider this: Positive actions are your legs of life. They keep you moving forward. When you damage your legs, you can't go anywhere. When you have strong legs, you can go somewhere to fix your bleeding hands, as in the analogy written above.

Did you notice in the paragraph above that I wrote "positive actions" and not "positive thoughts"? As I mentioned yesterday, you don't have to *think* positively to *do* positive things. Furthermore, your positive actions can be simple and small. Once you start doing positive things, your brain will eventually help you by producing positive feelings. You will start on an upward climb to recover from deflating thoughts.

I am writing this with the intent to help people that are feeling as if they are drowning in a negative world, whether it is because they feel bad about themselves or because they feel bad about their circumstances. The suggestions regarding white-blood-cell experiences (day 64) are not going to solve your problems. Implementing them is going to help your mind start finding answers. Your brain will not be able to work well when it is under stress. So

1. take a deep breath, start focusing your thoughts and actions on unstressful things, and

2. continue to do positive actions until you can begin to think positive things.

Positive thoughts can be as simple as "It is a sunny day," "It is nice to hear the birds," or "My feet feel comfortable and warm." Some people may think these suggestions are silly, but I've had to use these examples before. Sometimes focusing on a picture of something that brings about positive thoughts helps. I've done that as well.

I don't have negative thoughts bombarding my mind as I used to. I moved from ignoring them to replacing them, and then to having only positive thoughts.

Many psychologists recommend using affirmations. These are positive phrases about ourselves or our lives that we write and regularly recite. We don't have to believe they are true. They are dreams and hopes. They are positive, so they will induce reactions that translate into hope and peace. These are true-self feelings; dwell on them. Look over your true-self model. Picture yourself doing what you wish to do. Picture yourself where you wish to be. Picture the type of person you wish to be. When you are fighting an invader, do this often. When nonself thoughts come about, reflect upon the things of true self. You don't have to do anything; just think about your goals. You don't have to be all you want to be; just dream about what you will feel when you have improved. Replace nonself thoughts and wishes with true-self ones.

Keep building on the activity of looking at, thinking about, or reading something positive until you can think positively about yourself.

Take some time today to write positive things about you and life. It does not matter whether you believe them. Post these in various places.

Antibodies to remember are as follows:

- Negative thoughts, as true as they may be, will never, *ever* help me.
- Depression is regression.
- When I'm feeling blue, I can find something positive to think or do.

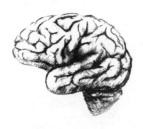

Day 66

Today I will (*after* you read your paper brain and self model!) introduce a specific invader to attack:

"This is too difficult for me."

There are moments in our lives when we are required to do things that leave us feeling worried or even panicked—moments when we think life just couldn't get any harder or we're asked to do things that are too challenging for us. Knowing the difference between something that is going to refine us and something that is going to cause us emotional or mental harm is tricky.

Knowing I'm going through a "refining" experience doesn't make going through the experience any easier. It just assures me it is okay to keep going.

When you find yourself in a refining circumstance, take time to meditate and reflect upon the beneficial aspects of what you are experiencing. Commit yourself to a deeper study of good books that offer wise counsel.

Antibodies to remember are as follows:

- When I think "I can't," I will add "but I can learn."
- Good is in my future, I will find it everywhere. It takes baby steps to steadily get me there.

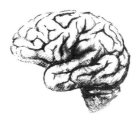

Day 67

Improvement is all about change. Today I will share ideas to attack this invader:

"It is impossible for me to change."

All too often, we fall prey to habits that hinder us. Perhaps the habits started out as curiosity or were undertaken to avoid embarrassment among friends. It may have continued as a means of getting rid of feelings of loneliness or heartache, or to avoid problems. If the habit is hindering you in some way, change is needed. And change is not easy on the brain. So how are you going to fight a habit that is hindering you? Whether the habit is constant negative thinking or an action, the habit is recorded on some strong neurological circuits—especially emotional circuits that are tied to a rewarding feeling. The exact science of your habit I will not go into, but I do want to note that the limbic system—which involves the emotions—is very automatic; your prefrontal cortex is not getting much of a chance to think through your actions or thoughts. This is important to understand to attack the problem of nonself habits. You will have to wire some new brain circuits. This is the process:

1. Decide on a replacement for the behavior. Write your replacement goals or thoughts on papers. Place these in

multiple spots so you will see them constantly. Place them in your room at home, in your car, and in your locker.

2. Use stress balls to fight the pain.

3. If the habit is tied with a setting or event (for example, while you are with certain friends or while watching TV), make plans to avoid that circumstance. It is so important to have a plan in place.

4. Begin by delaying the habit. There are two ideas for this:

   a. Think "Not right now; later." Wait five minutes the first time. The next time the temptation comes about, wait ten minutes. In this way you are building up the ability to make better choices. Eventually you can think "Not today," and then you can stretch it to "Not these few days." As you show your body that you can survive without the reward of your habit, you will gain greater ability to say yes to your life.

   b. Don't concentrate on avoiding the reach for the sweet treat or harmful substance; concentrate on keeping your hands in your pockets or holding an object for a certain amount of time.

Today I've explained specific ways to address the invader of habits. This has not addressed the underlying reason you may have a habit, but these ideas will help. These suggestions are not enough for deeply rooted addictions. Use the paper brain to create the type of life you want to live, and seek additional help so you can follow the new life you want. It will take a lot of effort to teach your brain what is important. That is, after all, what breaking a habit or addiction is all about: teaching your brain what really matters to you.

The antibody to remember is as follows:

- It is not in the snap of a finger that change will come your way; it is in the simplest of acts performed each day.

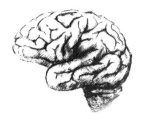

Day 68

Fatigue. Hunger. Irritation. Sadness. These are dangerous states of being that make it doubly hard to attack this invader: "I just can't resist …"

Over the last week, I've taught you about how to fight negative thoughts and feelings, or "nonself." Temptations are also a part of nonself. Temptations are opportunities that look appealing but are destructive in the long run. How do you face these?

Face, or attack, temptations by focusing on your ultimate goals. You can also apply ideas for the "It's impossible for me to change" invader I talked about yesterday. If you have some particularly tough temptations to avoid, write your ultimate goals on Post-it notes all around you: in your locker, near your bed, and near your dresser. Instead of attempting to resist an appealing opportunity or experience, be committed to your ultimate goals. Think, "I'm building a smart brain" or "I am too smart to fall for this."

Remember: if you are aware of tempting places or people that might try to tempt you, plan how you can avoid these circumstances and how you will respond to others' wishes.

Pay attention to your state of being. If you are hurried, hungry, hurting, or headed downhill, stop and think before you purchase, participate, discuss, or digest.

The antibodies to remember are as follows:

- This is only temporary bliss.
- I am too smart to fall for this.

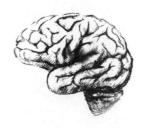

Day 69

You are nearing the end of this seventy-five-day journey. How are you feeling? What challenges do you have?

Discussing the antibody for today's invader may be very critical right now. The invader I will be covering is

"This just isn't working."

As you reflect upon your journey, keep in mind that progress and improvement take time. I told you back near the beginning that truth exists, and one important truth is that *progress takes time*. Don't believe the lies "It isn't working" and "It's not worth it." Your brain doesn't know the final outcome; how would it know that something isn't worth it or whether it's working? Your brain does not know the amount of time it takes to change or achieve your goals.

History is full of stories of inventors, explorers, entrepreneurs, and social activists who faced many obstacles and setbacks. It is true that progress takes time, but it is also true that an idea or plan will not come to fruition just because we show grit. Benjamin Franklin invented lots of things. He also attempted products that flopped in the marketplace.

This is an important invader to discuss, because having grit, being tenacious, and having endurance are important. However, some projects (can I mention the Edsel again?) need to be dropped. So how do you know the difference, and once you do, what do you do when you start to feel it is a failure?

When you start feeling this way, take these steps:

1. First, review the criteria for recognizing an invader (day 52). Is your idea enhancing to your life, helping to you or others, refining for you, and motivational? If it does not meet these criteria, it is nonself.

2. Let's say you have a goal that meets all these criteria, but it still feels as though it is just a plain "bad" idea because it isn't working out. Now ask these two questions: Do you fear you will lose money you can't afford or don't want to lose? Do you fear you will waste time? If either is the case, continue to step three.

3. At this moment, you need to research and talk to people. Do you have the basic skills to achieve your pursuit of a relationship, talent, or career? Is your goal financially sound? What help or words of wisdom can you get from others? Looking at your skills, plans, and resources with another person will give you an objective perspective to consider. Others' opinions are not more valuable than your own, but talking with others will give you information that can help you make a solid decision.

4. After your reflections and research, make a decision and write down what you learned. If your brain has doubting thoughts again, you will have concrete and true information to combat the doubtful thoughts with.

If you stop pursuing a goal, do so because you know it is the right thing to do for you, not because you just can't do it anymore. Please don't give up. Adjust the serenity prayer a little:

God,
Grant me the serenity to accept what I cannot do,
The ENURANCE to do the things I can, and
The wisdom to know the difference.

We cannot do all things in a lifetime. That is a fact. I cannot build a Tesla (though my son wishes I could). Still, having obstacles and taking a long time does not define what we can or cannot do.

After I've reflected on my goals and circumstance, and I know deep in my soul that my goals are right, I apply two antibodies when I encounter problems: (1) "For every problem, there is a solution," and (2) "I'm going to prove this won't work." No, the second one is not written in error. If I'm not feeling as though it will work, I choose not to argue with my brain's analysis of the situation. I decide instead to just go ahead and prove it right—that it won't work. Doing so keeps me going. Eventually, I see how the goal will be able to work.

Both of these challenges keep me in the game until I feel better. Do you see how I'm relying on my paper brain to decide how I will feel about doing something? I say to myself, "Okay, yes, you are warning me that this isn't a good idea. Maybe it isn't. But this is important to me (it is on my paper brain), and I'm going to figure this out even if it takes longer than I think."

The antibodies to remember are as follows:

- "I'm going to prove that this won't work." (Then give it your best shot to prove your point!)
- For every problem, there is a solution.

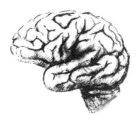

Day 70

The last phase of the immune system is the memory stage. This is a valuable stage because it allows us to fight certain foreign substances faster than we would otherwise be able to. Let me give you some details about this stage.

Memory and Antibodies

Sometimes antibodies attack; these antibodies attach to a virus and disable it. The body doesn't know what invaders are out there, so it produces thousands of variations of puzzle pieces. When one fits the job, it is replicated to eliminate all the microbes. The fitting piece is then saved for future times. In the future, the antibody will be ready to immediately go to work, and time will not be wasted as the body searches for a match.

In life, problems can sometimes be solved or prevented by applying lessons we have learned. Remind yourself of these lessons when old, nonself circumstances and thoughts creep up. Reflect upon your progress and the positive results you've experienced.

Don't let memories of past mistakes drag you down. Use them as a tool to help you in the future. The physical immune system has unwanted stuff coming at it all the time. It doesn't get discouraged; it simply fights what doesn't belong there and keeps on working.

What lessons have you learned so far in your life? Write about your life experiences in a way that is positive and that shows what you have learned. How will this experience help you or others?

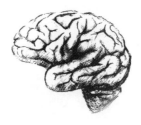

Day 71

Your body and brain function with the help of the nutrients you feed it. It is a pretty miraculous body, and it can survive on whatever you give it. However, because it is biological, it needs certain things for its varying responsibilities. Your body and brain function optimally when they have what they need. There are differing beliefs about the amounts of foods the body needs for basic function. It is undisputed, however, that your body needs water, a variety of fruits and vegetables, calcium, protein, and grains.

Furthermore, your body will function better with regular exercise. Make eating a proper diet and regularly exercising goals if it they are not goals for you already. You can add this to your paper brain. For your body (and brain) to function properly, it needs to be taken care of. Because nutrition is a critical part of a healthy mind, I highly recommend that you study about it. Are we to give up if we are not eating as we should? No! That is a deflating thought. Instead keep it on the paper brain wish list and don't forget about this goal.

Use this day to look up information about your health. Are there goals you would like to add to your brain wish list?

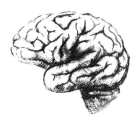

Day 72

You have just learned how to build an immune system for your soul.

1. Establish true self.

This means to identify and discover what you really value, believe, and wish to be.

2. Recognition Stage

Once you know what you want in life, you must learn how to recognize the thoughts, circumstances, behaviors, habits, goals and actions of self and others that prevent you from getting or being what you want. You learned to ask yourself four key questions:

1. Will it motivate or deflate?
2. Will it help or hinder (self and others)?
3. Will it refine or burn?
4. Will it enhance or distract?

Everything that is true to you will motivate, help, refine, and enhance. Avoid all others.

3. Strengthen external barriers.

External barriers prevent behaviors and thoughts that are nonself. Traits that are examples of external barriers are humor, faith in self and others, patience in self and others, gratitude, forgiveness, humility (teachability), and determination.

4. Attack with white blood cells

Outnumber the negative thoughts with positive thoughts, actions, and experiences. Following your brain model should help do this, because your true self is nothing but positive. However, unpleasant things will happen; it will take time to completely act according to your paper brain. In these cases, focus your attention on what good you can do. This does not mean we must ignore important issues and circumstances. It means that we want to keep the positive things at the forefront in our lives so we can deal with the negative appropriately.

5. Memory Stage

Remember what you have learned from both your mistakes and triumphs. Apply these principles when appropriate so you do not waste time trying to solve a problem you have already solved before.

6. Take care of yourself.

Eat well and exercise regularly.

In the beginning, I said that I wanted you to know what it means to develop an effective prefrontal cortex and to biologically record what you truly want. I also said I would explain the importance of these things and how to do them. Creating the paper brain helps you biologically record what you truly want. Following the immune system of the soul helps you take control of your limbic system and use your prefrontal cortex in a beneficial way.

As you recognize the things that thwart you, you use your working memory to pay attention to the stimuli your brain is receiving or processing. You take the time to decide whether something is important by activating all neuron connections to make a decision; you don't make the decision based on whether or not your brain has a strong emotional attachment to some of the choices.

When you consciously take the time to remember and use what you have learned, you create and strengthen new pathways.

As you regularly evaluate your external barriers, you are also create new pathways and reinforce old ones that you want to strengthen, especially when you consciously use them.

As you develop new behaviors to outnumber the negative, you strengthen the pathways of your true self.

The whole point is to be the true you and accomplish what is best for you in the end without any more effort than necessary. The way to get there is by thinking with your eyes. You have created several visual models of what you are and what you want to do. Think with your eyes often by studying your paper brain and the list of external barriers. In time, your brain will help you with these goals.

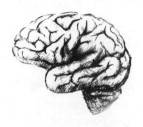

Day 73

Can you see the light at the end of the tunnel?

Today I want to examine these three questions that combine much of what has been presented in these pages. These questions help me a lot.

1. What is my perspective?
2. What is the truth?
3. Which thoughts and actions will help me?

Let's think about how these questions help. Answering the first two questions prevents us from reacting in a negative way.

For example, let's say one of my friends does not respond to a text or DM. If I expected to hear back immediately, I may first feel anxious and think something is wrong.

I can stop and ask, "What is my perspective? What is the truth?" Perhaps my friend is super busy. Maybe she is, in fact, upset with me or doesn't care. I don't know what the truth is until I find out. Now I ask, "What thoughts and actions will help?" I can choose to wait and see later how my friend is doing.

But what if I find out my friend is upset with me? Again, I can ask, "What is my perspective? What is the truth?" Can I talk with my friend? If not, does her attitude toward me change who I am? What is true about me and my life? What is true about my friend?

My heart may feel heavy. If so, I might ask, "What thoughts and actions will help me?" These are the "white blood cells" I wrote about on day 64. Helpful thoughts may include "My friend is not perfect," "This is not a reflection on me," "I'm not perfect either," and "I can make it through this." Helpful actions may include sharing how I feel with someone else to express myself or doing something nice for my friend or someone else. It will take effort to be positive and to apply the emergency white-blood-cell experiences, but as you do so, you will be feeling with your brain and not your heart.

You can do this.

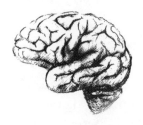

Day 74

Because truth is both helpful and important, today I would like to share some truths about the period of life you are experiencing.

Psychologists have named certain phases in human development, such as the terrible twos. When first married, couples experience the honeymoon phase. The article "The New Science of the Teenage Brain" found in the October 2011 issue of *National Geographic* points out that adolescence is not a Western culture phase of life. Culture may influence the length of adolescence and the behaviors of teenagers; however, all cultures recognize that there is a period in which human beings are more apt to be risk takers, seek the novel, and thrive on excitement.

All these stages of life can be explained by science. This fact was a little depressing to me as I realized that my own behaviors and thoughts are simple science. Am I just a robot? In a way, we all are. All behavior is a result of the brain's analysis of a stimulus (something that it sees, hears, feels, does, smells, tastes, or senses in some way). In this book, I've tried to help you triumph over becoming a robot programmed by society.

To fully understand ourselves, we need to know that every action we make is a result of a hundred billion neuron connections that have been set up over the years of our lives. Early in our lives, walking was not easy for us. You and I had to learn to do that. Our brains had the desire to get to someplace, and they pushed us to learn to walk.

Please remember that your brain is designed to make living easy for you. It doesn't like tough and unrewarding things. It will accept tough and *rewarding* things, however, because it *loves* rewards. Your brain is designed to drive you toward what it determines to be the best solution for feeling good. What feels good and what is easy—that is exactly what your brain wants for you. Two perfect goals for the brain to pursue are happiness and a pleasant life!

There is one big problem: at birth, your brain has as much understanding of what truly brings about happiness and a good life as it does calculus. Yes, your spirit recognizes all truth. However, at birth we don't automatically know all truth and have not developed the ability to *follow* all truth. The brain is not omniscient. It is not wired with great ability and knowledge from birth. It is, however, wired to seek rewards from birth, and it is designed in such a way as to make living easy. It is designed to be influenced with minor but repetitive stimuli.

You can repetitively "feed" your brain minor influential stimuli (what you read, think about, look at, and so forth) and begin to wire abilities and knowledge that will influence your behavior for good.

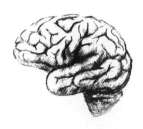

Day 75

You made it! Retake the following quiz to find out whether you are programming yourself now or whether your life is programming you.

1. Do you set goals?

    No.—0
    Yes. —1
    Yes, and I write them down. —2

2. If you set goals, do you reflect on them regularly?

    I wish I had the time or could remember! —0
    Yes, I think about them. —1
    Yes, I regularly think about my plans and what I'm doing.—2

3. Do you seek to learn how you can be a better person?

    Sort of. —1
    I actively try to be the best person I can by regularly reading or participating in things such as church or positive groups. —2

4. Do you act according to what you *know* is *good*, overcoming obstacles?

    No one is perfect, so of course we will all falter at times. On a scale of 0 to 2, how easily are you discouraged?

5. Sometimes events and words of others come to us unexpectedly—some good, and some not so good. Consider your reactions. Do you react to things conscientiously?

   I often regret the things I quickly say and do. —0
   I *try* to control my initial reactions. —1
   I am doing fairly well at slowing down and thinking about what is best.—2

The higher your score, the greater your awareness of your behavior and your efforts to choose actions that will benefit you in the long run. Compare your score with your score from day 1. Did the score increase? This is a time of reflection. Why did or didn't your score improve (increase)?

This is a time for reflection for me as well. Using feedback from others that share their journey results (the scores and their feelings), I can consider ways to improve the wording of this course. I welcome your input.

In this journey, I have been

one voice

sharing

two skills

(how to think with your eyes and feel with your brain),

three questions

(What is my perspective? What is truth? What
actions and thoughts will help me?),

four traits

(humility, reflectiveness, open-mindedness, and dedication),

and

five habits

(thinking, writing, reading, smiling, and overcoming).

Remember: we are overcoming negative forces in our lives. We are not in competition with other people. And there is a higher power—to me, God—that will help you in overcoming challenges and reaching daily moments of happiness. I wish you luck on your continued journey.

Resources

Audesirk, G., and T. Audesirk. *Biology: Life on Earth*, 4th ed. Upper Saddle River: Simon & Schuster, 1996.

Diamond, M., and J. Hopson, *Magic Trees of the Mind*. New York: Dutton. 1998.

Doman, G. *Teach Your Baby Math*. New York: Simon & Schuster, 1979.

Alkon, D. L. *Memory's Voice: Deciphering the Mind-Brain Code*. New York: Harper Collins, 1992.

August, P. N. *Brain Function*. New York: August-Chelsea House, 1988.

Begley, S. "Your Child's Brain." *Newsweek*, February 19, 1996.

Blakemore, S., and Robbins, T. "Decision Making in the Adolescent Brain." *Nat. Neuroscience*, 2012.

Covey, S. R. *The Seven Habits of Highly Effective People*. New York: Simon & Schuster, 1989.

Dobbs, David. "The New Science of the Teenage Brain." *National Geographic*, October 2011.

Fiorillo, C., and Tobler, P. S. "Discrete Coding of Reward Probability and Uncertainty by Dopamine Neurons." *Science*, 2003.

Johnson, S. "Emotions and the Brain: Fear" *Discover*, March 2003.

Khalsa, D. S., and C. Stauth. *Brain Longevity: The Breakthrough Medical Program that Improves Your Mind and Memory* New York: Warner Books. 1997.

LeDoux, J. *Synaptic Self: How Our Brains Become Who We Are*. New York: Viking Penguin, 2002.

Nash, J. M. "Telling Right from Wrong." *Time*, November 1, 1999.

Peoples, L. L. "Will, Anterior Cingulate Cortex, and Addiction." *Science*, 2002.

Richardson, S. "When Memories Lie." *Discover*, January 1997.

Robbins, J. "Wired for Sadness." *Discover*, April 2000.

Schultz, W., Dayan, P., and Montague, P. R. "Substrate of Prediction and Reward." *Science*, 1997.

Seligman, M. E. *The Optimistic Child*. Boston: Houghton Mifflin, 1995.

Somerville, R. *Emotions: Journey Through the MInd and Body*. Alexandria: Life-Time Books, 1994.

Van Dijk, S. *Don't Let Your Emotions Run Your Life for Teens*. Oakland: New Harbinger Publications, Inc., 2011.

Vogel, G. "Scientists Probe Feelings behind Decision-Making." *Science*, 1997.

Endnotes

1　Josesh LeDoux explains this in his book *Synaptic Self: How Our Brains Become Who We Are*.

2　Gretchen Vogel, in the article "Scientists Probe Feelings behind Decision-Making," writes of studies exploring the correlation between our choices and rewards and punishments.

3　To learn how traumatic experiences take control of thought processes and behavior, read Daniel Alkon's article "Memory's Voice: Deciphering the Mind-Brain Code."

4　To learn more about emotions and their effects, see articles by Steven Johnson in 2003's March, April, and May issues of *Discover*.

5　For more information about this story, see Audesirk's book *Biology: Life on Earth*, 4th ed., pp 713–722.

6　You can read amazing stories about brain recoveries in Glenn Doman's 1979 book *Teach Your Baby Math*. He founded the Institutes for the Achievement of Human Potential. Learn more at https://www.iahp.org/.

7　https://www.liveabout.com/the-edsel-a-legacy-of-failure-72601.

8　An abundance of literature is available on the effects of our environments. For parents of young children, I recommend reading S. Begley's article "Your Child's Brain" in *Newsweek*, February 19, 1996, and "Guns, Lies, and Videos" by K. Weight in the April 2003 issue of *Discover*.

9　For details about the physical manifestations of expectations or predictions, read the article "Discrete Coding of Reward Probability and Uncertainty by Dopamine Neurons" found in *Science* magazine, March 21, 2003.

10　Many books have been written about choices, thought processes, and their effects in our lives. Two that I recommend are Seligman's 1995 book *The Optimistic Child* and Covey's 1989 book *The Seven Habits of Highly Effective People*.

11 After studying the body's immune system, I developed the immune system of the soul in 1998. Ideas for the external barriers came from personal study of scriptures and religious leaders of Christianity.

12 Proverbs 17:22 KJV: "A merry heart doeth good like a medicine, but a broken spirit drieth up the bones."

13 Proverbs 3:5–6 KJV: "Trust in the Lord with all thine heart; and lean not unto thine own understanding. In all thy ways acknowledge Him, and He shall direct thy paths."

14 Romans 8:25 KJV: "But if we hope for that we see not, then do we with patience wait for it."

15 2 Corinthians 9:6–7 KJV: "But this I say, He which soweth sparingly shall reap sparingly; and he which soweth bountifully shall reap bountifully. Every man according as he purposeth in is heart, so let him give; not grudgingly, or of necessity; for God loveth a cheerful giver."

16 James 4:10 KJV: "Humble yourselves in the sight of the Lord, and He shall lift you up."

17 Matthew 18:21–22 KJV: "Then came Peter to him, and said, 'Lord, how oft shall my brother sin against me, and I forgive him? Till seven times? Jesus saith unto him, I say not unto thee, Until seven times: but, Until seventy time seven."

18 James 1:5 KJV: "Behold, we count them happy which endure."

19 J. Robbins, "Wired for Sadness," *Discover*, April 2000.

20 The ideas listed in this section are recommendations found in the following books: *Brain Longevity* by Dharma Khalsa and *Don't Let Your Emotions Run Your Life for Teens* by Sheri Van Dijk.

Printed in the United States
by Baker & Taylor Publisher Services